Peter Harris founded A Rocha after three years working in a parish on Merseyside, UK. Together with Leslie and Wendy Batty and their family, he and his wife Miranda with their three small children moved to Portugal in 1983 to establish and run A Rocha's first field study centre and bird observatory on the Ria de Alvor. In 1995 the work was given over to national leadership and they moved to France where they worked with national and international colleagues to establish a similar centre which opened early in 2001. Since leaving Portugal they have also been coordinating an emerging network of A Rocha projects which are now found in eighteen countries worldwide. The story of the first ten years of A Rocha is told in *Under the Bright Wings*.

'The story of A Rocha is a unique and inspiring epic. It brings with it a new wave of hope that religious believers will join scientists and environmentalists, including those who are secularists, to create a global movement with a real chance to save the living world.' – **Edward O. Wilson**, Pellegrino University Research Professor Emeritus at Harvard University and Honorary Curator in Entomology at the Museum of Comparative Zoology.

'Peter Harris is a persistent and most convincing witness that the Christ who saves and the Christ who creates are one and the same, that the care and celebration of creation is essential to a full evangelical witness of the gospel of salvation. If you are not yet convinced, please, read *Kingfisher's Fire*.' – **Eugene Peterson**, author of *The Message*

'For over twenty-five years I have been an enthusiastic supporter of A Rocha, and of their practical and educational work around the world. They are, in my judgement, a very fine organisation which is worthy of our strong support. I am delighted that my dear friend Peter Harris has now continued the story of A Rocha's pioneering mission in the pages of *Kingfisher's Fire*.' — **Revd Dr John Stott**, CBE

'Peter Harris has provided visionary and prophetic leadership and has given refreshing and effective models through A Rocha's network over the past twenty five years, reinforcing again the place of the gospel in all facets of life. These models are of great value to the conservation movement and in equal measure to the church. In *Kingfisher's Fire*, the A Rocha experience is creatively narrated.' – **Stella Simiyu**, Programme Officer, Global Strategy for Plant Conservation

'We believe that philanthropy is an investment in change, rather than merely letting the coins hit the bottom of the tin cup. Investing in sustainable development must take into account what's happening to the environment. A Rocha takes a holistic perspective on these issues. The thing we like most about A Rocha is that they are both advocating better care of the environment and are actually modelling it through their field programs, and study centres around the world. In *Kingfisher's Fire*, Peter Harris has given us an honest and compelling account of their work and approach that should be required reading for donors, investors and students of sustainable development.' – **Steve Beck**, CEO of Geneva Global Performance Philanthropy

'Like the Kingfisher in the poem from which Peter quotes, this book is his testimony. "Crying what I do is me: for that I came". With poetry, parables and prophecy Peter tells the story of how God laid it upon him, Miranda and the A Rocha family to follow in the footsteps of both the first and the second Adam and do God's will with the earth.' – **The Rt. Rev. James Jones**, Bishop of Liverpool

As kingfishers catch fire, dragonflies dráw fláme;
As tumbled over rim in roundy wells
Stones ring; like each tucked string tells, each hung bell's
Bow swung finds tongue to fling out broad its name;
Each mortal thing does one thing and the same:
Deals out that being indoors each one dwells;
Selves—goes itself; myself it speaks and spells,
Crying Whát I do is me: for that I came.

Gerard Manley Hopkins

Kingfisher's Fire

A story of hope for God's earth

Peter Harris

MONARCH
BOOKS

Oxford, UK, and Grand Rapids, Michigan, USA

Material from this book was presented to the London Lectures in Contemporary Christianity, 2007.

First published in the UK in 2008 by Monarch Books
(a publishing imprint of Lion Hudson plc),
Wilkinson House, Jordan Hill Road, Oxford OX2 8DR.
Tel: +44 (0)1865 302750 Fax: +44 (0)1865 302757
monarch@lionhudson.com
www.lionhudson.com

ISBN: 978-1-85424-848-0 (UK)
ISBN: 978-0-8254-6182-8 (USA)

Distributed by:
UK: Marston Book Services Ltd, PO Box 269, Abingdon, Oxon OX14 4YN;
USA: Kregel Publications, PO Box 2607, Grand Rapids, Michigan 49501

Unless otherwise stated, Scripture quotations are taken from the Holy Bible, New International Version, © 1973, 1978, 1984 by the International Bible Society. Used by permission of Hodder & Stoughton Ltd. All rights reserved.

This book has been printed on paper and board independently certified as having come from sustainable forests.

The environmental costs of this book have been met through a payment to Climate Stewards, www.climatestewards.net

British Library Cataloguing Data
A catalogue record for this book is available from the British Library.

Cover illustration by John Busby.

Printed and bound in Great Britain by Cox & Wyman Ltd, Reading.

For our first, dear grand-child, Alexa.

As our generation hands God's earth into the care of

yours, may this book bring you hope.

Contents

Foreword

When I think of A Rocha and read this text I am reminded of the mustard seed parable. This story, told by Jesus, teaches that a small work of God can grow into something larger and more significant, and this has certainly been the case with A Rocha.

> *'The kingdom of heaven is like a mustard seed, which a man took and sowed in his field; and this is smaller than all other seeds, but when it is full grown, it is larger than the garden plants and becomes a tree, so that the birds of the air come and nest in its branches' (Matthew 13: 31-32 NASB).*

A Rocha has seen enormous growth from the small seed that Peter and Miranda Harris planted at Cruzinha in Portugal. This growth has helped many birds to nest safely and brought about environmental benefits in places as diverse as the Aammiq wetland in Lebanon's Bekaa Valley, the forests of Kenya and a city park in Southall, London. The Kingfisher is only one of many species of birds to have found places to nest thanks to the dedicated work of the A Rocha team. As the environmental crisis has deepened it is heartening that the Spirit has moved and Christians around the world have listened and responded to his call to take better care of creation.

The story of A Rocha is also a lesson in patience. This book shows how the seed of a hidden work in Portugal, patiently carried out, suddenly germinated into an international organisation working in eighteen countries – it was certainly time to update *Under the Bright Wings*, Peter's earlier book. I now think of A Rocha every time I see a Kingfisher.

I have had the privilege of visiting the work of A Rocha in Portugal, India, the UK, the Czech Republic, France and Canada, and have personally seen how dedicated all the staff and volunteers are in their commitment to Christ, to creation and to the community in which they work. It is good that the work of some of these heroes of the faith is so well documented here. What is also impressive is the many different niches into which the A Rocha community has grown – the work is as varied as each of its eighteen national organisations. Above all, they are united in their faith and desire to do something that addresses the human-caused environmental mess in which we find the world.

This book is not just a fascinating account of the work of A Rocha and its many fine associates; it is a challenge to do more. Above all, I hope it will encourage and mobilise Christians around the world to take better care of God's creation, whether by participating in the work of A Rocha, or in that of other Christian organisations.

Professor Sir Ghillean Prance, FRS
Former Director, the Royal Botanic Gardens, Kew

Acknowledgements

First of all, I want to thank the A Rocha family around the world. I am honoured and grateful that they have allowed me to write about their story as I have seen it. This is also my opportunity to thank all those others who could not be named in person. In addition, I have had to change a few names to protect identities and places.

I am grateful to no less than six editors who have contributed their time and unique talents to *Kingfisher's Fire*.

Carolyn Armitage first encouraged me to write this book, and then never lost faith in it, even when it seemed it might never be finished. Thank you, Carolyn: without your sacrificial ministry, practical encouragement, and perceptive direction this writing would never have seen the light of day.

Since Barbara and Richard Mearns first came to find us in Vila Verde in 1984 they have been dearly valued friends and colleagues. Thank you, both, for the many hours you gave to reading each of these chapters, and for all your invaluable comments and improvements to the early version. I hope that all those who are awaiting your next book, a remarkable tribute to the American ornithologist John Kirk Townsend,[1] can forgive me for diverting your energies and talents just as your decade of dedication to honouring his memory reached its final stages.

American readers can be grateful to Maurice Irvin for generously working through the manuscript so that it could make more trans-Atlantic sense. It was doubly difficult as he also had to battle with all the Portuguese and French syntax that is now hard-wired into my sentence constructions.

Nathan Lemphers was another North American reader, generously coming from Vancouver to Les Tourades to work as my assistant par excellence for most of the time that this book was being written. Nathan, your locked-tight administrative and logistical skills simplified my life on many occasions over the last couple of years – thanks! It was your candid feedback that helped me see how this book might be received by anyone from MIT with dread-locks.

Miranda was not only the final editor and arbiter, but put aside her own writing so that she could give her entire support to this project. Her love and companionship on this journey, as on so many others we have taken together over the last thirty-one years, have blessed me beyond measure. Where next?

Prologue

I am not the only person for whom a Kingfisher has brought its startling fire to sluggish streams.

For a number of reasons, I was drawn to the bird for the title of this book. I wanted to give an account of a Christian movement which has now taken many remarkable forms in all kinds of places around the world, becoming in the process a bright sign of hope to believers and others alike. Careful and honest observation of all such phenomena reveals that they are made up of flames and muddy water in almost equal measure, but by recalling the Kingfisher's fire I can give it a name that will do justice to both.

As I searched for my title, I began once again with Gerard Manley Hopkins' poems, as I had done for *Under the Bright Wings*[1] which told the story of our early and sometimes tumultuous years in the south of Portugal. My wife, Miranda, and I had been joined by many others as we set up and ran a field study centre called A Rocha, whose name means The Rock. But we had no idea when it all began in the early eighties that it might give rise to a kind of global movement. We were simply living in an old farmhouse called Cruzinha with the daily challenges posed by life and work in a rapidly degrading semi-natural environment and struggling to see in practice what Christian convictions could bring to the work of environmental research, education and campaigning. Hopkins' prescient and passionate writing, his own highly personal response to the ravages that he saw being daily visited by the industrial revolution on the increasingly silent landscape and wildlife of Britain, spoke for our own vision of the beauty of all we saw around us, and even more for our appalled gaze on its rapid devastation.

For me personally, Hopkins' attachment to Wales and to the west of Britain has always given his poems a particular resonance. Miranda grew up near its cliffs, and since she introduced me to its wide horizons it has been the second home of our imaginations. Honesty compels me to admit that there were moments during our early visits together when she might have nourished the suspicion that her parents' home was too near the cliffs for the more traditional idylls of courtship – it didn't take long for this particular ornithologist to find a Peregrine's eerie a few minutes' walk from the house. So we were introduced, only too soon, to the particular romantic challenges that are necessarily implied by an immoderate, if less equal, passion for watching Raptors in a westerly gale or during long hours on frosty mornings as the Peregrines hunted down the Thrushes that migrate south in fugitive groups along the slate-dark coast. Years of growing love for this most beautiful of landscapes, even more than the joys of birding, have caused Pembrokeshire to become a second home to me as it was always first home on this earth to Miranda.

Quite apart from Hopkins' birds, we had our own reasons to be grateful to Kingfishers during the years at Cruzinha. On hot summer afternoons, visitors often arrived hoping to see a demonstration of the bird-ringing of which they had heard rumours in the cafés or market of our local village of Vila Verde. But we knew that any sensible bird would be hunkered down in the deep foliage of an olive or citrus tree out of the blazing heat.

Happily for the ongoing work of convincing the doubtful, there was often an obliging Kingfisher on one of the shady perches by the pool that we had established in the garden. Even more happily, it seemed to prefer a spot just at the mouth of a large Heligoland trap that we had constructed for migration studies. A brief stroll towards the catching box was usually enough to ensure that before long, everyone was entranced to see the phenomenal azure plumage of this jewel of a bird as we gently took it in our hands to put on a ring or check its age. The occasion that one was caught bearing a ring from the Czech Republic soon translated the episode into legend and finally established the wisdom of ringing over hunting in village mythology.

Some years later, the Kingfisher acquired new significance for us through a story told by Dave Bookless who, with his wife Anne and a growing team, has been pioneering the A Rocha work in London for the last decade. In the early days, he spent some time introducing local people in Southall to a derelict area of waste ground which held tremendous possibilities as a country park for the whole community. He told me recently of one particular morning there and a kind of epiphany. He had brought a young boy whose life had taken many wrong turnings to the site, hoping that somewhere in the bleak wreckage of his current circumstances it could give a small vision of other possibilities.

'We walked around, and after a while stood together on the bridge over the polluted stream. He seemed to appreciate the stillness and the space where he could just be. Suddenly a Kingfisher flew beneath us. The lad gasped at the astonishing brightness and beauty as the first bird was followed by a second, piping shrilly, and then a third, until five Kingfishers had flown under the bridge – a complete newly-fledged family party. Initially he was almost speechless, although when we got back he couldn't stop talking about it. Something had changed – the Kingfishers were like a touch of God's Holy Spirit bringing colour and a sense of special presence in the middle of everyday urban life. Whereas in the Gospels the Holy Spirit came as a dove, and to the ancient Celtic Christians the Spirit was the wild goose – beautiful and free, to us in the grime of urban Southall, God came as a Kingfisher.'

Finally, Eugene Peterson in his remarkable book *Christ Plays in Ten Thousand Places*[2], has given us further insights gained from Hopkins' clarity about creation. Among them is his use of the phrase 'Kingfisher life' to describe the complete integrity, the wholeness of being and purpose that is the true heritage of those who embrace a faithful relationship with Christ in all things. As he reads Hopkins' poem, Peterson sees how life in Christ should take hold of every part of our being and how it can truly be the conscious and unconscious force of all our lived experience.

That would be my prayer for everyone involved in A Rocha as we continue on our own journey, which is essentially and simply a common life given over to worshipping the Creator and so serving the creation. That worshipping life, at its best, is lived out even in the most deliberate and painstaking of daily choices, in field studies, or in the most arduous and unrewarding of ordinary chores that are the stuff of everyday work for environmental restoration. It is a life that is now lived all over the world by many different people who are intent on restoring their relationship to the creation as a consequence of their Christian worship. A 'Kingfisher life' is a fine way to describe the bright beauty of this vision that we glimpse in unpromising places.

As I write I am struggling to understand one of those curious moments in life – it seems too strange not to mention but I couldn't begin to explain it. I had just decided to risk telling a group of A Rocha friends in Kenya the title of this book when only a few minutes later there was a sharp tap on the window. We looked outside to discover a stunned Pygmy Kingfisher lying on the ground. We examined it carefully together, and as the photo shows, it is truly the most beautiful of creatures. After a few minutes recovering in a dark box it flew off in a blaze of azure and orange. I suppose that is part of the story that follows, then – all that goes on in creation colliding with what we have put there too, our part in both its damage and its recovery, the chance to see it closely in God's good time.

So, for all these reasons, it is my fervent hope that the Kingfisher's fire may continue to light up the efforts of all those who are working to sustain God's creation. Kingfishers stand as a special sign for the myriad other creatures that an African friend has well named 'The Big Five and the Small Many'. She meant that none should be overlooked because all are given over to our care and protection.

Chapter One:

The Landscape

O the mind, mind has mountains; cliffs of fall
Frightful, sheer, no-man-fathomed. Hold them cheap
May who ne'er hung there.[1]

Gerard Manley Hopkins

Markku Kostamo knew that visibility was poor on December mornings in rural British Columbia, but even so he was sure that last night he had left only seven cattle in his pasture. As he rubbed his eyes against the early gloom, he could see that there were at least forty there now, and they were a far more mixed bunch than his beloved Scottish Highlands. Heavy with the early dew on their hides, they were chewing philosophically and didn't seem in any hurry to go anywhere. Even so, Markku saw he had no alternative but to stumble out of the farmhouse and make a new plan for the morning. One quick look at the animals and a couple of phone calls later, he had his explanation.

Markku and his wife Leah run the farm in Canada as an A Rocha centre and among their neighbours is a cattle feed-lot. It was their entire stock that had made a break for freedom, quite wisely heading for the good organic pasture of the A Rocha meadows.

As an A Rocha experience, it was only too familiar and

disorientating. When the story of the first field study centre was told in the pages of *Under the Bright Wings* fifteen years ago, there was only one project to show for ten years of local involvement in the Algarve – one cow in the meadow as it were. At the time of writing, work is going on in seventeen countries. As just one indicator of what that means, I was recently told that over fifty thousand children were involved last year. Another seven national groups have joined in during the two years it has taken to write this book and more seem to be arriving all the time. It seems that God has opened the gates of our own particular meadow, and at times it causes us to rub our eyes in amazement.

Our own family has lived these last fifteen years partly as protagonists but mostly as almost incredulous observers of how one small environmental initiative in the south of Portugal could have given rise to a worldwide family of projects. I could have attempted to chronicle the journey earlier, but we have always believed that the A Rocha story is better told through being lived rather than by any talking or writing. Furthermore, it has been a story which is more authentically lived by a few people in a particular place rather than being told in an abbreviated version at a conference, or even through the pages of a book. However, with so many different local expressions of the A Rocha vision now having an impact and with the foundational notes of the vision now finding a resonance with so many people in so many different cultures and contexts, it seems as good a time as any to take the telling of the A Rocha story further.

At the outset I need to put the challenges into some perspective, and another backward look may help. As a student in the early 1970s, I arrived one summer evening at a small hotel near Loch Crinan on the west coast of Scotland looking for a job. The manager was clearly unimpressed, perhaps not surprisingly given the regrettable student hairstyles popular in Cambridge during those years. It is also possible that my failure to find any washing facilities during the long hitch-hike north was sufficiently evident to play a part in his first unfavourable impressions. But staff shortages had made him a desperate man and, after some haggling about the minimum wage – featuring, as I recall, some complex side deals about the daily number of the hotel's toasted sandwiches which might be counted as legal tender – he agreed to take me on to wash dishes.

There were no staff quarters available, but I was simply glad to stop travelling, and so I walked up the hill behind the hotel in the gathering night and the strengthening Scottish rain to pitch my tent. It was only the next morning when I pushed open the flap and emerged to blinding sunshine that I discovered that the site I had chosen lay on a grassy promontory, surrounded on every side by vertiginous falls. The cliffs upon which I was perched gave on to a wonderful prospect of headlands and islands, glistening sea and rocky shores stretching away endlessly to the beckoning west. In the drizzle and darkness of the previous evening I had been unaware of it all and had seen no further than the ground at my feet.

As I begin to give an account of this calling to care for the little we know of creation, the precipices seem only too present, and the beauty of the horizons appears at times too distant and too heartbreaking. The loss of the species and habitats that represent God's wisdom in creation is almost unbelievably rapid and the difficulties faced by the Christian communities who are now given to their restoration and protection seem as steep as the lines on the graphs which chart their rate of disappearance.

Meanwhile, fellow Christians are sometimes unpersuaded that we ought to care at all, whether they live in societies where they are unthinking guests at a feast of unsustainable consumption or whether they live in poorer communities. It has not escaped the notice of even casual secular travellers to such impoverished places that our poor theology is deeply problematic. Paul Theroux recounts in *Dark Star Safari*,[2] his unflinching saga of a journey from Cairo to Cape Town, an encounter with Helen, a Kikuyu missionary to northern Kenya. He hears her sing:

> *Marango pa nana!*
> *Shumata tengopai!*
> *Na ti lytorian – ni!*
>
> *(This world is not my home!*
> *My home is in heaven!*
> *Where God is!)*

and comments wryly, 'With that promise you were conditioned to brush off the years of drought, the poor harvests, the abandoned schoolhouse, the damaged borehole with its trickle of water.'

In Kenya only last week, visiting the rapidly fragmenting Dakatcha woodlands near the east coast, I heard that Christian communities and development organisations are among those who are responsible for the imminent ecological collapse that is already causing widespread hunger. Unless solutions are quickly found, the effective desertification of the area is inevitable. So their possible conversion to more biblical ideas of stewardship is probably the last hope for both the people and the place.

The same hope could exist for many other parts of the world if Christians can find their way back to the true consequences of their believing. Talking of his own country, the United States, the eminent biologist E.O. Wilson has said, 'The vast majority of Americans are Judeo-Christian, many of those are evangelical, [and they] are unconnected to the problems of conservation, especially global conservation, the loss of ecosystems and species which we have so well documented. It's too remote to them...'[3]

He and others who have been equally clear about their own lack of Christian faith have shown some courage in reaching out to evangelicals to seek co-operation in a mutual enterprise for the sake of biodiversity.[4] When asked what he hoped for from 'the religious community', he replied,

> First and foremost, numbers. Take, for example, the 30 million members of the US National Association of Evangelicals. If only 1 per cent of those decide that they really would like to add conservation to the way they act out their religious beliefs in the world, that's 300,000 new conservationists. That's overwhelming. The other reason is passion. Moral passion is what most evangelicals bring to the table. They believe, they care, and they really will work according to their beliefs. I think that having the living environment on their agenda for serious consideration and protection, with scientists playing the role of fact-gatherers and expositors of the problem, could be an extraordinarily strong combination. I'm optimistic. [5]

E.O. Wilson has accurately represented both a problem and an extraordinary opportunity. We only have to consider, for example, the millions of acres currently in the care of Christian farmers across the world. Just how much could change if they gained a greater awareness that how they farm the land is an expression of their relationship with God? Most already have a sense of responsibility for the social impact of their work that stems directly from their faith. A similarly intentional reflection on the tools they use for their work – from the machinery to the chemical armoury – can have a dramatic effect on the biodiversity found on their land, on the patch of God's creation that is in their care. In recent years I have talked with many farmers around the world who belong to all kinds of different church traditions, from Baptist to Mennonite, Catholic or Anglican, African traditional churches or Pentecostal, and nearly all have told me that this has come to them as a completely new idea.

The possibility that the care of creation could become second nature for Christians is in sharp contrast to the rather more limited scope of faith with which I was presented in earlier years. In the spirituality of the time it was more usual for the material dimensions of life to be seen as a distraction or worse. The general idea was that Christians should get as little involved as possible with what was going on around us and certainly not with anything environmental; it held no significance because we were living in what was only a (regrettably messy) waiting room for heaven.

It seems far more normal now for Christians to be profoundly engaged with both local communities and, increasingly, with local places. We have seen many quietly remarkable expressions of Christian living around the world that seem to encompass a more grateful and, quite literally, earthed walk with God than I ever knew was possible. It is this rediscovery that Bishop James Jones has called 'the earthing of heaven' as he takes us back again to the Lord's Prayer to remind us how often we say, 'Your kingdom come on earth as in heaven.' [6]

Many of the churches and Christian organisations with whom we have spent time during the last fifteen years of travels in many different countries have been places where human relationships, however broken or beautiful, are embraced in all of their complexity. This deeper level of personal encounter inevitably leads people to be more connected to their times and places.

It seems that the church is regaining the vision of the Psalms for every living thing around us so we are able to see creation as a kind of wordless speech from a loving Creator. It is part of a song, part of a bigger symphony of worship, given to us to know and care for. This is a long way from seeing creation as merely wallpaper for the more important story of personal spiritual fulfilment. As this vision captures our imaginations the bright horizon is nearer all the time.

As a practical result of this stronger Christian hold on creation, there are now physical landscapes, in both cities and rural areas, which look quite different after some years of backbreaking work. There are even places such as the Arabuko-Sokoke Forest in Kenya or the Aammiq wetland in Lebanon, the Ria de Alvor in Portugal or the Minet Park in London, that have been quite literally shaped by a true belief in a loving God who cares about the whole enterprise. As a direct consequence, the communities around and within them are living differently too.

The reflections in this book take place against some familiarity with the boundaries of my own tribe of Christian, which is typically labelled evangelical. In many parts of the

world this migrating term has become something of a night-
mare, and much firewood has been easily collected from its
wilder woods by those who enjoy the flames. Even so, more
reasonable definitions are not too hard to find and I can live
with the now famous quadrilateral offered by church historian David Bebbington,[7] recently summed up in suitably
technical fashion by Timothy Larsen in the Christian review,
Books and Culture, as follows: 'Bebbington defines evangelicals by their strong commitment to the Bible, the cross (that
is, salvation through the atoning work of Christ on the
cross), conversion, and activism (mobilizing the whole community for evangelism, missions, social work, and doing
good generally).'[8]

The true heritage of those who subscribe to this basic
set of convictions is being recovered after some decades of
disastrous dualism which took those core commitments
and removed them from their context in time and space.
There is plenty of evidence that life in Christ, understood
in truly biblical terms, can lead us to renewed relationships
with, quite literally, everything and everyone around us. It
is the creativity, energy and simple right living that a fully
biblical gospel makes possible which is the beauty of the
horizon ahead. Not only does it offer true hope even for the
endangered societies, places and species of the earth, it
opens up the prospect of more profound justice for the
poorer communities that depend upon them for the essen-
tials of their lives and who are suffering most acutely from
their current abuse.

But there are plenty of sheer falls, too, between us and
our horizon. So, well-tutored by the pessimism of the Latin
cultures in which I have lived for the last twenty-five years,
I need also to point out some of the precipices that we have

encountered on our journey and which lie ahead for A Rocha, as for many others.

The first is particular to secular Western cultures. It seems to be increasingly difficult for us to find some common ground where Christians and others can work together on issues that concern us all.

One tried and tested way that we deal with inconvenient animals is to domesticate them, and Western society has been domesticating Christians for centuries. In some societies the cages that have been provided are quite well appointed but, whether luxurious or oppressive, their aim is to keep Christians well out of the traffic. In our absence, environmental concern has quite reasonably become the province of brisk and successful secular organisations for which 'religion' has been typically understood as a social option (just like bell-ringing or bridge). So the belated appearance of evangelical Christians in the field has caused some moments of mutual confusion and even comedy.

'Good, we have always wanted to get to the Pope. Any chance you could organise it?' has been perhaps the best of a number of memorable responses that I can recall from initial meetings with environmental CEOs. In fact, now I think of it, this yearning to get to the Vatican seems to be shared by a surprising number of the most hard-boiled secular professionals. Either way, I fear that on a continuing acquaintance with A Rocha, people tend to discover that we are disappointingly uninterested in church hierarchies. We are, on the other hand, frequently intrigued by the convictions that are entertained by even the most avowedly secular of our partner organisations or donors. They usually prove to be religious in character if not in labelling and always deserve further exploration.

Christians can sometimes seem as ready as their more intemperate critics to stay behind the barricades and lob hostile projectiles of invective at those they have identified as the enemy. In response, their more ingenuous opponents are not above claiming the most extreme spokespeople as fair representatives of the Christian approach to the environment. It is hardly a promising start for joint action on a task that is vitally important for all humanity.

But on the edge of this precipice we can recall that a belief in a shared creation implies an understanding of inevitable community. The possibilities for that community of the created are at the heart of much that we have always hoped to do. In consequence, even in writing this book, I retain the hope that it can be possible to speak to both a secular and a Christian audience although our current fractured culture means that some demands must necessarily be made on the patience of all. Many good questions from both sides reveal the differences – partners and friends of A Rocha who would not identify themselves as Christian tend to ask, 'Why bring God into what are surely just technical issues? Can't we just keep our focus on the budget and on the species outputs?' Questions from Christians are more likely to be concerned about the social impact of our work, and whether we can talk about Christ as we undertake our projects. But all are good questions, and the attempt to keep working on them within one social space is well worth making.

If the search for common culture is increasingly fraught with falls, the need to find common language leads us to the edge of our second precipice, because we must use the word 'creation'.

The church has devoted an enormous amount of energy

in recent decades to internecine wrangles about creation's origins. When A Rocha's vision was first introduced to Christians in Peru, the USA, Bulgaria and Finland, this question immediately proved problematic in different ways but we were sure that creation's present acute distress ought to relativise the importance of in-house wrangling.

It is our observation that the controversy has been a scandal to uncommitted or sceptical observers in the scientific community, and a sterile distraction for the church itself. Not only have many public exchanges been notably polemic, but they have often been conducted by protagonists who lack the relevant disciplines of biblical studies, philosophy, and the life sciences, and they have been dogged by a persistent lack of cross-disciplinary understanding. Thankfully, the recent encounter between leading scientists and evangelicals which prompted E.O. Wilson's appeal – and fortunately a number of those involved were both – began by agreeing that this particular discussion need not be found at the top of the agenda whenever they engage with each other. [9]

A third precipice remains to be negotiated. It was first identified by the historian Lynn White but, because he found it en route from a false trail, Christians have failed to listen to his more important criticism. He argued that even if Christians claim to value creation, it is hard to see anything particularly different about the way that they live their beliefs.

Theology has come a long way in the decades since he first accused Judeo-Christian ideas of dominion of being the root cause of the ecological crisis.[10] His article, and the crisis itself, provoked Christians to look again at our heritage of stewardship. As we did so, we noticed very quickly that he was wrong to locate the problem in the nature of Christian belief itself: even foundational ideas such as our being made in the image of God imply a call to care for creation. So, as Fred van Dyke has pointed out, White did the Christian world a favour by causing us to rediscover the relevance of our beliefs about creation, and what they truly are. 'It was, in fact, the spark that ignited the developmental fire of the modern Judeo-Christian environmental stewardship ethic, the one that Callicott and others now recognise as 'especially elegant and powerful.'[11]

In passing, I have to say that the Christian world has done Lynn White a favour in return by keeping his essential accusation going for some years beyond what might normally have been its shelf life, given the rather shaky historical and exegetical foundations on which it was constructed. A ritual exhumation of his arguments seems to have become de rigueur for the early paragraphs of any writing about Christianity and the environment. I am giving my own nod in White's direction, not because I feel I must observe convention, but because we need to take better note of what is obvious to him: what we believe must make a difference to how we live.

I believe that he was right to suggest that Christians have been complicit in many environmental and social ills, but I believe it is because we have abandoned, or ignored, our biblical beliefs about the creation, rather than that they are ill-adapted to ecological life on earth. In reality, it is Christian belief itself that calls us to respond to the current massive, worldwide loss of species.

Since White's original article appeared in 1967, the global situation has deteriorated even more dramatically. Estimates vary, but it would seem that the current rate of extinction could be at least five hundred times faster than normal, and we could lose more than 35 per cent of animal species in groups such as amphibians or larger mammals in the next fifty years.

As Christians respond to a catastrophe on this scale, we need to begin by confessing that this is new territory for most of us. We have to acknowledge that, despite our Christian heritage and our professed relationship with God the Creator, concern for the creation is newer to us than it is to others. Many of those who do not share our faith have been more aware of what is going on in the world around us and more ready to live differently in consequence.

The next step is more demanding because merely bolting on an additional set of ethics will not suffice. The gospel makes it clear that it is only a change of heart and not simply behaviour that makes a difference; the only starting point for authentic Christian transformation is a restored relationship with our loving God. It is that renewed relationship with the Creator which will be our true road to a renewed relationship with his creation.

I am only too aware, as I embark on this account of A Rocha, of the many books already available on the themes I am addressing. My only justification for adding another to the collection is that each new exposition of belief adds to the need for some honest explanations of how it can work out in practice. So the purpose of this book is to describe what working for the healing of a world in ecological crisis has meant for a whole range of different people and communities. These A Rocha stories grow out of the grit of our own ground, from where God's good purposes have planted us.

We have found there are no blueprints and even fewer

markers that we can leave along the way, not least because the routes themselves have been so varied and, at times, serendipitous. God has clearly been involved in it all but equally clearly, for much of the time at least, we have had very little idea of exactly how or why. However, we have all believed that Christ's gift of new life for the world is meant to be lived, not simply discussed and declared. So what follows describes the consequences of our wavering and dimly perceived commitment to that life.

Precipices hold their terrors for those who don't see well, and our own present darkness should make anyone who ventures to write about these things cautious. By our own, I mean that of our times in the Western world: each day brings us a better understanding of the complete unsustainability of our way of living while adding little to our wisdom about what to do about it. Climate change has served to increase that uncertainty almost exponentially. All around us the normal fellowship of our existence, in the form of larks or squirrels, moths or frogs, is quietly taking its leave, and it is no exaggeration to say that the typical discourse of environmental people is characteristically lacking in hope. And by our own present darkness I also mean the personal bafflement of our own family, a sentiment apparently shared by many of those we know, wherever and however they live in this wide world that the Lord of Creation has entrusted to our care. Rich or poor, it seems we ourselves all participate in the sins and misunderstandings of our culture, and thereby often betray the very ideas about creation that we are coming to believe. None of this makes it easy to hang on to hope, however well grounded.

A penultimate difficulty in writing this story resides in

our personal circumstances. I have wanted to give an entirely candid explanation of the commitments of A Rocha as Miranda and I have lived them in recent years. But after twelve years spent in one place with relatively few people during our time in Portugal, we are now working in many different countries alongside many different people. The almost constant travelling has meant that we have lived too often in the anonymity of crowds. Even at home we spend hours at a desk, on computers or in meetings or, even worse, in the virtual meetings of internet conference calls. So for over half the year our personal landscape is a habitat of bus stations, airports and railways, inevitably punctuated, even in the poorest of countries, by stops in the globalised internet café – chosen venue for the worker without an office but never without a connection. For the other half of the year we battle to keep our home the place of community we wish it to be. Cables trail across tables, and papers are swept aside so we can prepare for unexpected guests who join us for meals that are then punctuated by phone calls. Steps are in hand, but even so...

There is the occasional story to tell even from such unpromising surroundings, and it would be interesting to write a book about reclaiming those spaces and relation-ships – we still believe in redemption. Either way, if what we had to tell now was our own personal story it couldn't lay claim to the romantic resonance of the earlier years, lived as they were with students at dawn on the Alvor marshes, or talking with fishermen at nightfall on the cliffs of the Ponta de Almadena waiting for European Storm Petrels to put in an epiphanic appearance. So what follows will be more like small fragments of adventures and expe-riences that have been lived more fully by many of our friends and colleagues in the A Rocha family.

And so to conclude this litany of Latin lament. We have lived for the last ten years in a French village, initially because it gave us a good starting point for a further A Rocha field project, and now because it has become home, however often we leave. 'Home', as T.S. Eliot wrote, 'is where one starts from.'[12] Living in this particular small village is a daily joy. It has no less than seven bakeries and five flower shops, and an inexhaustibly rich collection of local stories as told in contradictory versions by our much-loved neighbours Henri and Sylvanne. But there is so little to add to the vast library of English accounts of life in semi-rural France that I am only going to risk a few pages later on for fun and to honour Henri's huge enthusiasm for seeing A Rocha in print. Each day he scans the pages of La Provence, appearing triumphantly at the door with any new article that appears about A Rocha's activities in the valley. He was deeply gratified when Foi d'Ecolo (roughly translated The Faith of an Eco-Freak) appeared, finally bringing him *Under the Bright Wings* in a language he feels is proper to civilisation and at last providing him with an explanation of what his errant neighbours were up to.

So there is my thicket of difficulties, sketched in suffi-ciently foreboding terms to satisfy the most ruthless Alentejano pessimist; but like all such pessimists I will continue anyway, drawn on by a hopeless ideal. However hesitantly, I do so because we have discovered during the last twenty-five years of endeavouring to live out faithfully the convictions of A Rocha that many others are living them out even more persuasively in their own lives and work, both formally within a project, or quietly in their local lives. We have been greatly encouraged and helped in this common journey and wish to give a clear account of what is inspiring us all to continue.

After all, we now have colleagues in Beirut who have already given ten working years to the protection of Lebanon's fragile and beautiful wild places. They had twelve bombs within a mile of their apartment in the first few months of this year and then lived through a short war, dangerous flights across borders and traumatic evacuations. We have other colleagues in India who against all kinds of odds have mobilised over two hundred volunteers to patrol the boundaries of a national park so that the interactions of people and Asian Elephants can pass off peacefully instead of destructively. Others elsewhere have sold their houses to fund their work for A Rocha or for other Christian environmental initiatives. Many have lived with misunderstanding, threats or scarcely veiled invective. Commitment like that deserves an explanation.

We continue to be inspired by the growing number of Christians who live out their love for the Creator by working for the beautiful and beleaguered ecosystems and species of this earth. They do so because we understand that creation truly is, as our friend Graham McAll has put it 'this wonderful gift that we have been lent'. When working at our most clear-sighted, the love of Christ compels us, not the promise of success, nor even the hope of survival as a species if we get it right. We suspect we are part of something truly God-breathed, a way to love God the Creator by caring for his creation. It is a calling that can become second nature, the simple expression of normal Christian living and worship.

This caring for creation has spontaneously taken a number of widely varying forms, as could be expected of Christians who live and work in such a wide variety of contexts around the world. Almost daily it seems that new incarnations of the Christian life are taking shape in all kinds of different communities, in green or city spaces, in stands of rare trees or in new expanses of precious fresh-water wetlands. It is beginning to look almost too multi-coloured and creative to discern the common threads, but some shared commitments are emerging within the lives of many involved in this work and we would like to make them more widely known. They have to do with a closer hold on community, a deeper search for the relationships that must lie behind the tactics and techniques of the environmentally concerned. They appear out of the wisdom of different cultures renewed in Christ and are seen in the strength of his embrace of the broken-hearted.

Maybe, above all, the care of creation is an exploration of hope. Perhaps that is why it seems important to tell the A Rocha story as it arrives at this particular point. We can pass on our longing that many others could take these commitments upon themselves in their own places and times, given to be lived by the same faith. And we do so in order to explain ourselves to many of our friends, not themselves Christians, who have told us they wish to understand what is truly distinctive about a Christian approach to these issues which concern us all.

As Henri would say: 'Voilà!'

Chapter Two:

Picking Up the Portuguese Story

Insufficient Portuguese and a lively and efflorescent imagination combined to build up in his memory many very strange conversations.[1]

Rose Macauley

At the end of a spring morning in 1993, I hit the keys one last time on an ancient word processor that was still recovering from serial abuse at the hands of over-caffeinated students writing up their fieldwork well behind deadline. We were still living in Cruzinha, and the old farmhouse was running at all hours of day and night in an organic rhythm tied in to the tides of the Alvor estuary and the seasons of Mediterranean bird migration. The more prudent requirements of even the most rudimentary management theory might have suggested something different for all involved, but we loved it. We had been there for ten years by then. By the time we got round to writing the story on that word processor, a lot of people had become part of the work and the wide-ranging community associated with it and some hundreds of them had dispersed around the world. So it was that the vision which many people encountered for the first time at Cruzinha began to travel, and thus it happened that we are now part of a kind of worldwide family.

During those Cruzinha years we came to feel an almost physical joy in the sharp and bitter beauty of the Mediterranean landscapes with their unforgiving summer heat, hissing with the sound of the cicadas in the pines. We had even found ways of living with the all-pervasive damp of the warm Atlantic winters as it stealthily laid mould on the walls of the house and gently soaked the paper we wrote on. In spring, the botanists could hardly keep up with the profusion of plants that all seemed to flower within the first days of the warm air drifting up from the African coast; in autumn, successive waves of warblers and waders moved through the area on their way south, all challenging our capacity to record their various migrations.

We had moved to the shores of the estuary at the foot of the village of Vila Verde because it gave Portuguese students a wonderful opportunity to study a wide range of complex and remarkable ecosystems that were nearly all under imminent threat of destruction. An uncontrolled explosion of tourist development was transforming the coastal strip before our eyes and, inland on the serras, the original woodlands were rapidly being replaced with eucalyptus monocultures. It was our hope that we could bring the results of some solid research to the aid of those who were seeing an environmental catastrophe unfolding before their eyes, and who were beginning to look for a more sustainable future for both the local environment and its rapidly transforming villages and towns. Over the years, a lot of expertise and energy arrived to help the cause but it was getting to know the extraordinary people who brought it with them which gave us the greatest joy of all. They were of all ages and were soon arriving from many countries apart from Portugal, perhaps because of the particular Portuguese genius of welcoming all-comers with such instinctive hospitality and lack of pretension. Very soon each one of them seemed to find a way of becoming part of an ongoing effort to know the area better and to work for its protection.

Over the initial years of intensive studies we came to know the habitats well and began to understand something of the wealth of life they each contained. We even came to recognise some of their inhabitants quite precisely as ring-ing studies identified individual warblers that returned each winter to the same clump of pistachio bushes or to the same stand of olive trees. They appeared in successive years, returning from summer woods sometimes 3,000 miles away to the north. Other studies allowed us to follow the fortunes of the various European Bee-Eater colonies on the headland from year to year, and to see how the dynamics of the Little Tern and Kentish Plover colonies on the sand dunes were so finely tuned to their survival. It was this knowledge that became almost unbearable in the face of the casual destruction that was gaining momentum on every side.

In those few short years we learned to live with an insis-tent counterpoint to all the new discoveries. This other Algarve reality was marked by the draining of the last reed beds, the removal of most of the coastal dunes where endemic plants were tenuously making their last stand and the bulldozing of the remaining native oak woods. In their place incendiary eucalyptus plantations now cover the original living hillsides like silent graveyards. As we saw the sorry changes that the landscape was undergoing, we watched rural communities begin to disintegrate under the pressure of new aspirations. Who could resist the chance of a quick profit from the influx of millions of tourists who were arriving en masse on proliferating new roads and on multiplying budget flights?

It was the railway line that brought us far more encouraging signs of change in the form of growing numbers of Portuguese students. Over the years several became close friends and colleagues, almost family, and the story of A Rocha in Portugal has been theirs for the last decade. It began by our handing over the governance to a small group of friends from different parts of the country. At the outset they were catching up fast with this expatriate obsession with birds but were frankly more interested in the possibility of a decent lunch when the work plan and accounts had been approved. I don't believe that it was until after we had left and Mark and Jane Bolton had taken over the running of the centre that a truly national direction emerged for its work.

During Mark and Jane's tenure, Cruzinha's scientific programme made major advances and the buildings and grounds all underwent a serious upgrade. But it was in encouraging their national colleagues and in making way for the creative convictions of Alfredo Abreu and his committee that maybe they made their greatest contribution. The next stage of Cruzinha's development began when Marcial and Paula Felgueiras returned to take on leadership of the work there in the summer of 2000. Their extraordinary gifts for hospitality have given Cruzinha an atmosphere more typical of a home than a field study centre. Marcial and Paula, together with Isobel 'Bébé'

Soares who runs the environmental education programme, have been the core members of a team whose
incredible endurance has continued to protect the estuary
and marshes to this day.

A Rocha teams in many countries have intentionally
adopted some of the Latin ways of the first project at
Cruzinha and, in particular, a preference for giving time to
building relationships as their context for developing programmes of work together. Even beyond this indirect influence of Portuguese ways in many places, Alfredo, Marcial
and Bébé have been closely involved in the fortunes of the
emerging group in Brazil.

However, in the mid-nineties, as we handed over the
fortunes of Cruzinha to our Portuguese colleagues,
thoughts of Brazil were far from anyone's minds. It was in
the local context of the Algarve that they were applying
their energy and ideas. They were far more able than we
had ever been to understand the labyrinthine coils of local
and national politics that had complicated decision-making around the Alvor estuary and throughout the region.
They also had a far better understanding of the way that
our friends and critics in the local community perceived
the work of A Rocha.

As they gradually took on the direction of the work, they
fulfilled the long-held hopes of people such as Bob Pullan,
who had not only led the original Trustees in the UK, but
had brought the bio-geographical expertise of his department at Liverpool University to bear through a series of
original and important studies. He had known we were only
invited guests, however welcome, and that it would take
national leadership to really make the difference. Without it,
the results of all the fieldwork and reports would have little
influence in forming a wiser land-use policy.

The Trustees in England had always understood themselves to be caretakers, or midwives, of a project that would eventually be Portuguese in inspiration. So they began to meet more often with a small group of our friends from Evora and Lisbon around the long Cruzinha table for which Miranda had triumphantly sacrificed half of the original furnishing budget. It soon became obvious that this small group of Portuguese leaders could see clearly why A Rocha might be significant in the country's conservation and Christian worlds. They were only too aware that local decisions about land-use were simply echoing the choices now being made in wider society.

'The Algarve – your Personal Paradise!' proclaimed tatty hoardings at the side of the new motorways. Vitor Franco and the others who formed the first management committee for Cruzinha understood well that these highly individualised choices reflected very different values from those which had held together not only family and social life in the Algarve over previous decades but also the ecological balance of the region. They were far from nostalgic for life under Salazar's extreme right regime but they also understood better than we could how the materialistic priorities now evident throughout the country were marginalising even the vestigial Christian thinking that had been part of the culture until recently.

'Christians are beginning to retreat to the ghetto,' Vitor told us. So A Rocha seemed even more strategic to them than we had thought it could be. It was time to hand over the challenges to those who really understood them.

By the time we left, Cruzinha was annually welcoming over two hundred people to stay for periods of time that ranged from a week to a year. As well as those occupying the rooms and occasionally camping on the lawn, there were around a thousand day visitors each year, including regular school groups who booked in with first Rosário and then Paula, the pioneers of the national team. Violinda's cooking was an undeniable draw for the residents. It still is, but as the house approaches its twentieth year of grateful appreciation of her uncontested gastronomic prowess, people from all ranks of the environmental world continue to be drawn also by the store of treasures in the study area. Any interest in fieldwork that they bring can find a perfect match in a region which has been so little studied. Each month seems to bring something new to our understanding of this very special place.

One of our own early studies revealed that European Storm Petrels were coming to the coast on early summer nights, and by 1994 we were able to ring nearly 500 of these beautiful little seabirds in one season. Fourteen of them came bearing rings from further north and another ten were soon recaptured in Spain, Scotland and Norway. The study took on even more significance in later years under the direction of Rob Thomas from Cardiff University as he led a team that examined the impact of changing climate and sea temperatures on many aspects of the bird's life cycle. Even while I have been writing this chapter, news has arrived of the 4,000th bird ringed as the study now goes into its seventeenth year.

In spring and autumn there was often a spate of new national records of many taxa, and even a new species for science in the garden (a moth of the genus Hypotia for those who appreciate these things). The seasons were full of surprises, as can be expected when you take time to look at a largely ignored creation. Even in Europe, and even after centuries of enthusiastic observation, the smallest patch of ground can yield the entirely unknown.

With the huge enthusiasms of different people who joined the team through the eighties and nineties driving us on, the days had been long and the nights of sleep deeply eroded. Will Simonson had joined us straight out of Cambridge to develop the botanical studies and as people started to go further afield, we began to get used to them being stranded in sudden rainstorms in the Serra de Caldeirão or lost on the back tracks of the Monchique hills. Meanwhile, groups were out at night ringing waders on the salinas or catching seabirds at Arabida. Then, of course, on the way back home it made sense to check out the colony of Common Swifts in the abandoned factory at Chinicato or, even worse, to call in at the rubbish dump to look for gulls bearing wing tags or rings from the north. In any quieter moments there was data to enter on the increasingly numerous computers, or help was required to put up equipment for the next day's studies.

It was very exhilarating but, by the end of our time at Cruzinha, a certain fatigue was beginning to make itself felt, for me at least. Miranda, on the other hand, was now living within the very rich fabric of relationships that life in a village can give anyone who has an intuition of how God seems to feel about simply everyone. Nevertheless, we could both see that we were coming to a crossroads, and so we began to talk seriously about what our future might look like. If we had to leave to make space for our national colleagues to take over, did that mean we should leave Portugal altogether? Alfredo and I went prospecting in the north of the country to see if another site suggested itself for a new centre, but no joy. So, should we return to our original ideas of working in East Africa? But by then I had no adrenals or thyroid following surgery for some tumours that had appeared, and so the medics banned us from even considering it. We wanted to continue with the same kind of work, but suspected that our widening age gap from the visiting students left us less equipped for their robust ideas of how life could be fun in a residential centre; particularly one given over to the all-consuming demands of field studies.

We were also coming to believe that there is a limit to the time you can go on accumulating data about God's wisdom in creation alongside the evidence of environmental folly without becoming depressed. If you face acute uncertainty about a study site that you know and care for, exhaustion can become a real enemy. None of the reasons, taken on its own, would have caused us to leave, but together they pushed us towards taking a next step. Several current leaders in A Rocha will know only too well what I am writing about. In the final couple of years on the headland, I found that even the shortest survey became an ordeal and seemingly insignificant moments such as encountering a large Mercedes bearing men in suits driving down the lane, or reading a small and apparently innocuous newspaper article about the disbanding of a local planning committee, could lead to almost paranoid speculation. All too often the local rumours that were simply the coinage of village exchange triggered over-sensitive fears in me that the area had already been sold for rapid and disastrous transformation and that years of work would serve only as a memorial to a lost treasure.

But either way, whether out of relief in the discovery of truly wise national leadership, or out of the normal rhythm of the journey we had been on, it was time for us to leave.

As the summer of 1995 began, to the grief of our entire family, who by then had been profoundly and generously adopted into Portugal and its wonderful ways, we finally packed our bags.

Chapter Three:

New Beginnings and Early Dying

It just can't happen in our family
Even though a thousand
And ten thousand at your right hand.[1]

David Jones

We had hoped to have the 'arriving' part of The Plan as clear in our minds as the 'now we really do have to leave' part – but it wasn't to be.

Even before we had left Cruzinha, friends of A Rocha had, with the typical commitment of their kind, offered us the use of a splendid group of medieval farm buildings in the north of France. However, despite their beauty and eminent suitability, the miles of sterile agri-desert that surrounded it were enough to deter even the most dedicated birder determined to take an interest in any species he could find. Quite simply there was very little to be found apart from a few House Sparrows in the barn, a couple of depressed-looking Skylarks on a tiny remnant field edge, and a distant Common Buzzard clearly heading for the hills. There were kilometres of green landscape but they were as devoid of life as a superstore car park and the almost complete absence of any plants, insects or birds meant that reluctantly we had to decline the generous offer.

I have subsequently carried out a number of surveys on such habitats in France that allow me to affirm that this story is formelle, the official version. It is the local manifestation of a post-war wildlife tragedy affecting all the intensively farmed land of Western Europe, but happily one that is now showing signs of considerable improvement in some of the more wisely-worked areas.

There is an irony here. It now remains to be seen how much of the Eastern European biodiversity that was flourishing until very recently on traditionally managed farmland will survive the same narrow bottleneck of commercial ambition through which we have to pass in the West. In Bulgaria, Romania and the Czech Republic a similar corporate assault to that which ravaged the farmlands of Western Europe in the fifties and sixties is in full swing now. Behind it goes the end of human community and a deepening silence in the fields as dulled slabs of engineered and sterile green replace the astonishingly varied palette of the original pastures and put an end to all that lived in and around them.

Such a landscape would never work for the next A Rocha centre, but amid the ongoing Cruzinha activity we had never found time to look elsewhere. Apart from the brief forays to northern Portugal, and some unfruitful musing about sites we had seen on short visits with friends to Spain, Morocco and Turkey, we hadn't been able to come up with much. Life becomes complex for a family with four school-age children and the equal number of gracefully aging parents who were increasingly appreciative of our spending more time together. So, undeterred by the label of 'middle-age travellers' that our growing kids soon attached to us, we decided to embark on a series of visits to some of those who were wanting to talk about their hopes and plans to set up an A Rocha project in their own country. Maybe we could join them there? We had also been invited to teach in several places around the world, and it seemed a good idea to give our theology, and an account of its practical outworking, a wider audience and a more rigorous road test. So began a peripatetic existence that was to last for almost two years.

The first assignment was to visit Rogélio and Patrícia Hogg who had found their way to Vila Verde following an encounter in Buenos Aires with former Cruzinha visitors. They were among many who were by now arriving at the centre from far and wide. We had never put any publicity out there, but as Christians interested in conservation remained a rare species, so news of A Rocha was beginning to travel quite fast among the few who were.

In Rogélio and Patrícia's case it had been a long journey to our door. Rogélio had worked in the Iguaçu Falls National Park in northern Argentina, but he had then changed career to become an Anglican pastor in the community of Los Cocos near Córdoba. There he and Patrícia found themselves living in a former orphanage on the edge of an area of great environmental interest. The hills behind their home were part of a national park, and the landscapes around the town were beautiful, even though many of the trees were festooned with the plastic bags that the wind blew everywhere. 'Argentina's national flower,' Rogélio ruefully told us, although subsequently we have heard the same wry claim in several other countries like Kenya and Peru. The usual suspects of deforestation, overgrazing, uncontrolled burning and lack of planning controls, already so familiar to us in the Algarve, were rapidly degrading the local environment there too. Even so, rich biodiversity was clinging on wherever there were remaining pockets of viable habitat and not only did Rogélio know each place and the people responsible for it, he was also convinced that many of the people living around Los Cocos would want to join in a project to restore something of the area's former beauty and value.

And so their dream of an A Rocha project in Argentina had been born. In early 1995, with the support of their bishop in Buenos Aires, David Leake, they had come to see us in Portugal. We knew that they were kindred spirits as soon as we saw them cheerfully joking their way through an unpromising encounter with the famously grumpy customs immigration officials at Faro airport, a shakedown that ended amid laughter and back-slapping. In the days that followed we discovered that they were full of exuberant life, deeply involved with their local community and endlessly curious about ours.

It is true that their time in Vila Verde didn't get off to the most diplomatic of starts. We all went up to the village one evening to watch the Portuguese football team on the café television, only to discover Rogélio possessed a very Argentinian talent for commentary (think war, not sport). It perhaps showed a lack of imagination to go in the first place. Rogélio was completely unaffected by being a Spanish-speaking crowd of one and the atmosphere thickened ominously after he celebrated the first opposition goal at length and very loudly in the best Córdoba tradition. As his best idea for healing the breach after the final whistle was to encourage our friends in the bar to develop a taste for drinking the bitter maté which he had brought with him to celebrate, we had some ground to make up over following days.

They joined in with everything going on at Cruzinha with great gusto. 'Just whhatt made you decide to do this?' was Rogélio's constant question over the washing-up in the Cruzinha kitchen. We would rack our brains to remember and then struggle to convert our answer from Portuguese into wretchedly mangled Spanish. He and Patrícia obviously had plenty of energy and a clear vision for how their empty buildings could take on life as a field study centre. They were sure that a place like Cruzinha would be just what was needed to bring people together to start a new programme of restoration for the many degraded habitats around Los Cocos.

'If you would only come!' became their theme song, sure that visitors from a Latin project in Europe could be the catalyst to get people together to find a way forward for the area. We had spent some time in different parts of Africa and south-east Asia too, but South America would be new territory for both of us. So even though by now we were committed to a travelling life, we took a lot of persuading. However, by the autumn of 1995, when the three younger children were back in school again in the UK, we headed for Los Cocos, having stored the stuff that wasn't needed for the trip with long-suffering friends.

Our visit was eventful from the start, particularly as our hosts' generous provision of a fruit bowl in our room proved to be a poisoned chalice. We were staying in a hut in the former orphanage grounds whose roof harboured an impressive bat colony and during a violent storm on our second day, their droppings fell unnoticed into the bowl. I cannot make the story suitably biblical by implying that it was Miranda who gave me the fruit to eat but, at their worst moments, the consequences did seem almost Old Testamentally violent. So through the haze of subsequent bouts of gastric grief my memories of the lively social events laid on for us by Rogélio are less than sharp, but we were deeply impressed by all the plans taking shape in his energetic brain.

As he gave us a whirlwind tour of his favourite places and people, he kept saying, 'It could be A Rocha!' and 'See how it could work here!' It didn't take us long to be persuaded that he and Patrícia had found a way to give a new shape to the original A Rocha vision in an entirely different context.

In coming years we were to see this same phenomenon time after time, and to be astonished over and again at the endless creativity of God's family. There is a kind of beauty to be seen each time the gospel is lived out in yet another different configuration. We have seen it bringing hope to some very challenging places on earth, and yet in every one it is both the same and completely new.

The start in Los Cocos had been primarily the result of the strong relationships that Rogélio and Patrícia had built over the previous three years with a number of people who lived around the town and who were concerned by its range of urgent environmental problems. The small river that wound through the valley was being stripped upstream of much of the gravel on an entirely random basis. There seemed to be open season on many of the trees on the surrounding hills and, as a result, serious erosion was in full swing. Over-enthusiastic burning of the upland grass pasture, intended to stimulate new growth, was depleting the soil and affecting the quality of the grazing for the remaining livestock.

Whilst only a tiny minority were aware of how serious the problem had become, there was some hope in the fact that even in the small town of Los Cocos and, indeed, even the local church, there were some remarkably gifted environmental people. One such was Maurice Rumboll, an eminent ornithologist and a lay leader in the Anglican congregation. He was an imposing figure with a huge beard, and legendary among other things for his discovery of a new species, the beautiful Hooded Grebe, while he was working in Patagonia in 1974. He told us how he had sent his zoology students out to collect some specimens for a taxidermy practicum, and among the birds they brought in lay this black and white Grebe which he immediately knew to be a waterbird he had never seen before. He was even more sure that if he had never seen it before, after all his decades of fieldwork, no one had. Happily it didn't take long for him to be reassured that his students hadn't shot the last living specimen. A small population is still hanging on there now, even if the Hooded Grebe is among the more threatened species on a growing list of highly endangered birds in the region. As we looked over the photos and reports in his crowded office, he told us that he was urging on Rogélio and Patrícia in their developing enthusiasm to see A Rocha get established. He also assured us that he would do all he could to bring in others across the country to support them.

Maurice was not the only one around Los Cocos for whom a common passion in ornithology had been the beginning of a friendship with Rógelio. He had been getting to know a young couple of Marxist-Leninist persuasions, Luís and Cristina and, early in our first week there, he took us out of town to the shore of a small wetland to meet them. Despite their unambiguous atheism, they were great fans of all Rogélio was doing and as keen as anyone we met there to see A Rocha get started.

During a pause in his knowledgeable commentary on all the birds that were calling from a narrow rim of reeds around the edge of the pools, Luís told us more about the site.

'You may think this is a fantastic place, but you wouldn't believe the pressure to get rid of it for good. It's unique, claro, but I can tell you that Christian politics is all part of the problem.'

He and Cristina had been involved for some years in the effort to save the place from a series of threats from developers and, as the story unfolded, we heard transposed into South American tones a devastatingly accurate outsider's critique of dualistic theology. We listened with dismay to their account of the reactions of all their Christian friends, apart from Rogélio.

'They just say we should take less notice of what's going on here and concentrate on "things above".'

It seemed that this much misread text from the apostle Paul was no better understood in its Spanish version than it was in Portuguese, English or Swahili. Rogélio was indignant, and hopeful that we could help him put the record straight, so with the distractions of the birding over, we went back to their place in town for a late breakfast and some time to talk further.

As nearly always happens when Christians are able to listen to their critics, we soon found that we held far more in common than any of us might have suspected and it went well beyond a shared appreciation of the Pied-billed Grebes we had watched ducking in and out of the reed beds. It takes trust before people can share their deeply held feelings, and Luís and Cristina clearly thought we would be fiercely defensive of anything that was going on in the name of 'Christian'. We, on the other hand, were probably even more grieved than they were by their stories of backroom deals between evangelists and local politicians. Although we may have shared a faith in Christ, the personal financial empires that some Christian leaders were building, made even worse by their hollow promises of prosperity to desperately poor local communities, contradicted the real commitments of an authentic gospel.

'Their kind of message packs the halls, though,' Rogélio told us. For their part, Luís and Cristina were intrigued as he explained that actually Christians believe that being made in the image of God implies that people have a sacred charge to care for creation, not to destroy it. The conversation ended with an exchange that we have found very typical of such encounters.

Luís had said: 'We feel so angry. It is simply political and religious corruption that is causing all of the catastrophes around us here. And all we have to keep us fighting is our anger.'

And we found ourselves looking back at all the battles surrounding the Alvor estuary and saying, 'It may be hard to accept or understand, but we don't think there's any guarantee at all that things will work out the way we want. It seems to be a truly broken world and Christians aren't exempt from the consequences any more than anyone else as we live with what happens. We don't feel we can let up on the responsibility to care about it and then to try to do something. But the only thing that keeps us going is being grateful – just gratitude to a loving Creator. It doesn't seem that anything else, whether anger or a need to make it work out in the end, is enough for the long haul that you need to get anywhere.'

We left their place even more convinced that Rogélio's style of involving everyone from the local community in the discussions of what was to be a specifically Christian initiative chimed in exactly with the approach we had been trying to follow for years in Vila Verde and the surrounding towns. His dual role as respected pastor and able conservationist gave him a natural authority and Patrícia brought her own flair for hospitality to a compelling mix. Several of the others we met, particularly a dynamic young couple called Paco and Cathy, seemed to possess exactly the gifts and abilities that would be needed to create a healthy team and it all looked extremely promising.

So we returned to Europe full of excitement at the prospect of a second A Rocha project taking shape soon on another continent. There were lots of things that would need to be worked out, not least the extent of our own involvement, but the Trustees had made it clear that they expected us to give our time in coming years to nurturing and supporting new manifestations of the A Rocha vision. This Argentinian incarnation of the original ideas seemed to be a perfect beginning for the next chapter of A Rocha's life.

However, things were to transpire very differently from all we had imagined and hoped for together.

Rogélio had collected us at the airport when we first arrived. 'How are you?' is a normal enough greeting in any language, but even our limited Spanish was enough to tell us that his answer wasn't quite as we might have expected.

'Well, not too good in fact, but nothing to worry about,' was all he had said.

We hadn't given it too much thought in the hectic days that followed, as he had seemed as energetic as ever. So just four months later, we were stunned to hear from Patrícia that he had been diagnosed with cancer and then, just a few weeks after that, to hear from her again.

'This is the first letter that I have written since Rogélio's physical death – I want you to know very specially that the peace of God is with me. Although people look at me and the children as if we were strange beings we are truly calm and held up by God's help. The deep pain of losing Rogélio will never shake that peace from within us. He gave us the best of his life, and now only God will accompany us...' She was left with three young children to bring up on her own.

Our principal grief was for Patrícia and the family, but for all those at Los Cocos with high hopes for A Rocha it was a baffling and hard time too. Over the coming years we seemed to live a similar pattern many times – we learned that caring about people brings its own pain and mystery. We can make all kinds of plans but they seem more often than not to turn out differently from the way we see them. Even if they do go as we hope, they rarely do it at the pace we envisage. Furthermore, however promising the funding, or buildings, or ideas for new initiatives, it is the people who get involved who are always the true heart of it all. Without their commitment and without what we increasingly recognised as a shared DNA, there can be no possible journey together. Without Rogélio giving all his passion and God-given personality to the task, there was no heart beating for the infant A Rocha Argentina, and so all the planning came to an abrupt halt.

Patrícia has continued in Los Cocos and when Maurice's daughter came to volunteer in Portugal recently, she told us that the facilities at Los Cocos are still waiting to be put to a new use. Earlier this year, Alfredo met another Argentinian couple in Brazil, about to return to the area and considering whether they could take the vision on again, so perhaps the embers might flicker back into life after a decade of waiting. It would be remarkable if so, and that story will have to wait for the telling.

In the months that followed Rogélio's death, as we continued to travel, packing and re-packing the bags, we determined to carry with us this hard first lesson that A Rocha's growth would happen in God's ways. There was no shortage of different places to remember it in, as the weeks and months that followed were filled with ongoing conversations about potential new A Rocha projects, conducted via email on our newly acquired laptop. Despite the fact that it was a small and basic machine operated by the simple expedient of tapping its black and white screen with a pen, it served to keep us in touch with a number of people now working to see A Rocha established in new countries. South America wasn't the only continent on which the fires were being lit.

The flame was first carried to the wide open spaces of Africa by Colin Jackson who had made a big impact on the life of Cruzinha during the three years he had spent with us in the early nineties. Now working in the museum in Nairobi, he was finding that a number of Kenyan friends and colleagues were keen to see if there were any possibilities for A Rocha there too. As one door closed in Argentina, maybe another was opening in Kenya?

Chapter Four:

Under African Skies

Today, as in the past, Africa is regarded as an object, as the reflection of some alien star, as the stomping ground of colonizers, merchants, missionaries, ethnographers, large charitable organisations... Meantime, most importantly, it exists for itself alone, within itself, a timeless sealed, separate continent, shapeless little fields of manioc, jungles, the immeasurable Sahara, rivers slowly drying up, thinning forests, sick monstrous cities – a world charged, at the same time, with a restless and violent electricity.[1]

Ryszard Kapuscinski

Our daughter Jo had been the first to meet Colin on his arrival at Cruzinha. 'He says "ears" instead of "yes"!' she reported in delight, rushing up the stairs to our flat to tell the rest of the family. It was our first clue that he had been born and brought up in Kenya, and the children then applied themselves to the challenge of contriving questions that would get him to say it again, the first of many duels in the months and years to come. He joined the team in Portugal after completing an environmental science degree in the UK and his three years with us were marked by episodes of high adventure, major advances in our field programmes and a degree of creative chaos that presaged, even then, the likely pattern for his subsequent A Rocha career.

Typical of those years was the expedition he mounted to the island of Berlenga just north of Lisbon. He wanted to find out if European Storm Petrels were breeding there, as we had discovered they were visiting the mainland coast of the Algarve on summer nights, but they had never been recorded nesting. There was a well-established colony of Cory's Shearwaters among the barren rocks and his hope was that we could find a few of these smaller petrels coming ashore among them.

So far, so simple. He persuaded all the residents of Cruzinha at the time, around a dozen of us, to go with him. In the middle of the first night we had just returned to our dilapidated lodgings in the island's ruined castle when the darkness erupted in a drunken takeover of the buildings. It transpired that the intruders were a remnant revolutionary group who had chosen that night to come back over from the mainland and stake a claim to the place; we had no idea that such political passions still survived in peaceful Portugal, by then a regular European democracy. Our own conviction that we had an equal right to be there seemed suddenly quite pallid by contrast, but after some noisy exchanges featuring invective of the kind that would have been more familiar to residents of St Petersburg in the early twentieth century, we were relieved to see that alcohol was slowly gaining over rhetorical violence. Eventually relative peace was restored, together with an uneasy truce over our occupation of some of the castle's rooms that lasted for our remaining days on the island.

It was only one of the nocturnal adventures that

attended Colin's continuing quest for the truth about Storm Petrel colonies. His study involved going out to the coast with sound equipment and projecting loud recordings of the birds' calls over the waves. The general idea was that petrels would then be drawn to his nets so that they could be fitted with rings before they continued on their migratory way. So, shortly after the Berlenga trip, he was on the dunes west of Alvor, happily deafening himself and a small group of other visiting researchers, when suddenly, over the din coming from his speakers, he heard shots being fired out of the darkness into the air over his head. A group of local police arrived at a run, intent on his arrest, having quite reasonably taken the ear-splitting bird calls for the sound of a drug runner's boat making a fast getaway, a more familiar noise on the coast at that time of night.

Weapons had been fired and so once begun, the arrest had to run its course. There was a fine moment of farce after they had shoved Colin in the back of their jeep – the Guarda then had to borrow his torch to search for their ignition key which they thought they had dropped in the dunes during their stealthy approach. Colin earned some points when he found it under his feet in the back of the jeep; they then all set off to Portimão for a couple of hours form-filling, but in true Jackson style the episode laid the foundations for a friendship which proved of great subsequent value to us all. On a number of nights during other superficially ambiguous study expeditions out on the coast or marshes, a uniformed figure would loom out of the dark at the edge of the ringing site. 'Oh it's you again,' would be the invariable greeting of the intrepid Sergeant Pires. But, after a while, we suspected he only came for the coffee and some company.

Colin's passion for fieldwork and his exuberant enthusiasm for ornithology brought Cruzinha alive. Some of the irreverent nicknames he gave students and volunteers have stayed with them to this day, although as that is usually to their chagrin, it would be unfair to immortalise them in print.

His time with us in Portugal was also marked by the terrible day when the news arrived from Kenya that his brother Pete had been killed near Orus while volunteering on a rural project.[2] The way Colin and his whole family lived through such grief made a great impression on a lot of people, and if anything Pete's death only strengthened Colin's own desire to return home. It wasn't too surprising, then, that he also wanted to see if A Rocha's work could contribute to a country that was now doubly close to his heart. So two years before our own departure from Cruzinha, Colin left to begin his preparations for new work back in Kenya.

In what could be thought an unusual first step for a conservationist, he decided that his first months should be given to theological training. He was convinced that in Kenya, where Christian churches hold the allegiance of at least 70 per cent of the population, he needed to be well prepared to make the case for conservation to a potentially vital and influential new constituency. It seemed that very few church leaders had any environmental awareness or involvement and, to date, there had been little examination of what Christian stewardship might mean in Kenya.

A decade later his hard-won analysis is very widely shared and it seems as though a great awakening is taking place. A number of case studies have shown that in Kenya, as in very many poorer countries in the global south, the role of the churches is crucial in determining what happens to the local environment. At a Nairobi conference in early 2007, a series of examples given by speakers from both the Kenya Wildlife Service and the United Nations Environment Program made it clear that Colin had made a wise choice in giving time to understanding why Christians are natural conservationists. Several presentations suggested that secular conservation groups need to give more recognition to the role played by belief, and hence by the churches, in the decision-making of southern hemisphere countries. It was argued that as long as North American and European organisations assume that religion and society must exist in sealed compartments, they will be ill-equipped for effective work in societies where belief plays a central and unashamed role.

Even with all the potential that clearly existed for an A Rocha project, Colin discovered on his return to Kenya in 1994 that because relationships are essential, setting up a national organisation takes time. So, over the following four years, he worked at the National Museum in Nairobi as a research ornithologist, slowly gaining experience and building up support for his ideas among colleagues and friends, church leaders and scientists. He was also able to draw together a group of remarkable Kenyan advisors to form an initial steering group for the project, chief of whom was Edwyn Kiptinness, universally known as 'Kip'.

Kip cultivates a number of eccentricities for the amusement of his friends and often introduces himself by explaining, accompanied by extravagant mime, that his name means 'he who opens the way for cows'. He tells the tale of his Kalenjin father returning from a particularly successful night rustling the cattle of a local white farmer to discover that he had a new son on whom he triumphantly bestowed the name. According to Kip, 'All the cattle of the world belong to the Kalenjin – we were just getting back what is rightfully ours', but it doesn't take long to discover that his carefully cultivated tribal persona is only a front for highly sophisticated business acumen. Even more importantly perhaps, he had known Colin from childhood and so, some would say, has been quite able to cope with controlling an incorrigible pioneer who is quite genuinely wild.

Either way, he was just the person to give leadership to the group that he and Colin convened to set up the new A Rocha organisation. They looked for people who could cover all the bases of financial and NGO experience, conservation expertise and wisdom in the complexities of the Christian world. By the end of 1998, a national committee was in place and A Rocha Kenya became a fully-fledged entity. Shortly afterwards the decision was made that Colin should move down to the coast to explore the possibilities for work in the area around Watamu, just to the south of Malindi. He had already been involved in a number of research projects there and it was clear there was great potential for further useful work.

At first sight Turtle Bay Beach Club seemed an unlikely starting partner for an A Rocha project. Watamu is a place, like many others on tropical coasts, where acute poverty and a series of highly vulnerable and important habitats co-exist uneasily with a recent influx of wealthy visitors on holiday. Why this hotel was different was that they saw the possibilities that this juxtaposition offered for eco-tourism. This could provide a steady income stream which might be applied to relieving some of the urgent challenges. So when Colin asked if they were prepared to employ him to set up environmental and community initiatives they took him on immediately and he began to study ways of making a more sustainable connection between the hotel's visitors and the local area.

Once again the hard-won lessons of Cruzinha began to take shape in another country as the early months passed and Colin came to terms with all the complications of the local issues he was encountering. He soon began to get to know a wide variety of people whose lives were directly affected by all the environmental choices being made in the area by different organisations and interest groups. He spent many months listening and talking in the poorest of villages and in meetings with visiting scientists, with local pastors and politicians and with Nairobi-based business people. At one end of the scale he began to understand the acute local needs for school fees or a sustainable harvest of maize or fish and at the other the pressure people felt to find a life that they had only ever seen on television. In Watamu, crowds would gather at night, sometimes ten deep, to gaze at the shifting images on the small screens that had now appeared in many of the dukas and bars. These different aspirations seemed at times to be completely irreconcilable and contradictory. What was certain was that both the physical environment and the human communities that depended on its well-being for their survival were showing increasing signs of stress. There was no doubt that new approaches to very old and familiar dilemmas would be welcome.

He began by offering his own, by now considerable, skills in East African ornithology and then was able to bring in a growing number of volunteers to support the existing conservation projects in the area. Students from Nairobi and casual visitors to the coast were all drawn in to the initial work that was needed. Patient field studies started to make clear the tangled causes of many of the more immediate threats to the fragile and rare habitats around Watamu. As other project funding that had been the mainstay of work on several other sites nearby came to an end, A Rocha was invited to take up the relay. It was clearly essential for Colin to find a way of giving more of his effort to building a full-time team and to setting up a centre which could provide a home base for their work. His initial research period at the coast had lasted three years and, after the early periods of isolation, it would come as a relief to continue in a more established setting with local colleagues.

It was at this point in 1999, when our own pioneering days were over, that Miranda and I made our first visit to see what had been achieved so far and, to meet all of those involved both at the coast and in Nairobi. We were already finding common themes were emerging in each of the projects that were taking shape in the different countries we visited, but every situation was unique and we had a lot to learn. The warm humid air enfolded us as soon as we arrived at Malindi, together with an exuberant welcome from Colin and, it seemed, from a huge number of people that he now knew quite well. He had already been training bird guides, who were beginning to make a good living in the forest by showing visitors around. As we walked under the high brachystegia canopy in the cool early morning air, their sibilant whispers identified everything that we could hear, picking up on the most fleeting of calls. 'Amani Sunbird, East Coast Akalat, Sokoke Pipit...' It was a litany of the extraordinary, and we only hoped it wasn't a roll-call of the doomed, as all three, and a further three species that we didn't see during our short visit, are found only in this tiny area.

In the villages around the edge of the forest we saw the series of imaginative field projects that were being rapidly developed to address the need for sustainable incomes alongside food security. Many local families were completely stuck in a poverty trap and had been taking over land from the forest, desperately farming its shallow soils while they could, or even using the trees themselves in a hopeless one-way shot at generating some cash. As we went around together, Colin introduced us to his new friends and colleagues, many of whom were from the area. Through their eyes, in their homes and villages, we saw the depth of the dilemmas they were facing.

Although he was beginning to understand the urgent needs at the coast, Colin soon discovered that many of the important decisions for the area were made in Nairobi. Far too often he found himself taking the overnight bus to the capital, spending twelve hours hammering over the deep potholes on lethal roads to spend long hours the next day waiting in lines outside government offices. Permits were needed for everything and even straightforward transactions at a bank could take most of the day. If A Rocha was ever to grow, this was clearly never going to be a sustainable use of his time. We talked it over with the new committee and Colin's scientific colleagues at the museum in Nairobi and it was soon decided that they needed a base in the city to handle many of the logistics. Shortly afterwards Beatrice Kodhe joined the team as National Administrator and Colin was able to focus on the rapidly growing programme of research and conservation that was developing at Watamu.

A few weeks later Stanley Baya joined the Watamu team to bring much-needed coordination to the rapidly growing community programme, closely followed by Tsofa Mweni who took on the development of the new environmental education work. Both were highly respected local teachers: Stanley was particularly well known for his courageous stance against corruption which had cost him his job as head teacher of a local private school. In order to provide a home for their operations and to accommodate the growing number of volunteers from overseas who were beginning to arrive, Colin moved into a small two-roomed bungalow just south of Turtle Bay. Our son Jeremy had quickly made sure he was the first volunteer to move in with him and we were not surprised to hear in his first letter that Colin's only real concern about the place was that its garden would be suitable for bird-ringing. Sure enough the next letter carried a set of dramatic pictures of birds of prey being measured and ringed on the veranda.

No one could have foreseen at that point how the work would develop so strongly, both in Nairobi and at the coast. On a visit to Watamu only last month we met at least twenty people working with A Rocha, including Roni who married Colin in 2005. She has brought to the heart of the team her own very considerable gifts as a conservationist with experience throughout southern Africa. She has also brought a deeply grounded Christian faith. Nothing less could have equipped her for marriage to Colin.

From the days when A Rocha first began to put down its Kenyan roots, it was clear that all those involved would require unusual commitment. Two exceptionally gifted and influential leaders, Professor Jasper Mumo and Dr Tom Kabii, joined Kip, Stella Simiyu and Jasper Yego to form the first National Committee. Tragically and almost unbelievably, both were killed on the roads within months of each other.

There were setbacks in the form of corrupt officialdom, political instability and inter-religious tensions. In Watamu, as in much of the coastal area, Muslim and Christian communities lived closely together and wider global tensions combined at times with the local stress on resources to create real pressure. In addition, a random mugging and several robberies compounded the usual difficulties and complicated logistics that are familiar to all who live in the world's poorer countries. Watamu's population of Sykes' Monkeys was irresistible to visiting researchers but the monkeys' predilection for swinging on the phone lines made communications between the Watamu team and the growing group of A Rocha supporters in the rest of the country and beyond fitful at best. Thankfully, and not surprisingly, there were also times of great encouragement along the way. The story surrounding the centre that was finally established in 2004 was one of them. In order to see why it was so important to the future of the work at Watamu we need to step back a pace.

A Rocha has sometimes been understood as an organisation committed to incarnational action – that is to say, we draw a lot of inspiration from the way that Jesus lived out his message. He was effectively silent for the first thirty years of his short life, during which he learned to understand his times and culture, bearing its burdens and sharing the brokenness that confronted him on every side. Only after he had lived those thirty years in obscurity and reticence did he begin to preach the kingdom of God and to act publicly and visibly. We have concluded, following all the others who have endeavoured to live in his ways through the ages that anyone wishing to get involved in the rich fabric of any local community will need to embark on that kind of journey. It seems that truly transformational work will normally be built on very long-term commitments to particular places, in all their complexity.

This is just one of the reasons why setting up field study centres where people can live together is a central component of our conservation strategy: they become a visible sign of commitment to the area. Each one is designed to survive the vagaries of short-term project funding. We have seen how such centres can provide a context for profound relationships which can then develop with all those who get involved with the project itself and then with the communities around. We have seen how the common task of conservation, shared by the often unlikely combinations of people who contribute their skills and live in a centre, serves as richly relational ground for those who are ready to make the commitment to work with others. In turn, their long-term involvement in both the centre and in the local community can bring about a kind of renewal and restoration that goes well beyond the positive effects of even the most well-founded research and conservation programmes. It is a kind of negation of the heroic individualism that has at times been the dominant paradigm for many scientists but infinitely more rewarding.

These were the convictions that were woven into the story of this particular centre. For many years an indomitable British lady, Barbara Simpson, had run a reasonably basic guest house on the coast at Watamu. She had come to Kenya aged two, and then grew up, as coincidence would have it, on the neighbouring coffee farm to Colin's father, Julian. She was perhaps best known for her intrepid solo flight down the Rift Valley from England in 1930, piloting her two-seater Cessna just a week after gaining her licence. The flight ended when she made a crash landing on a Ugandan soccer field, but at least she had arrived in East Africa, which was more than she did on a subsequent journey, this time in a Morris Minor that only made it half way across the Sahara. She had travelled all over the region as an animal pathologist and, once settled on the coast, she lent her considerable energies to the support of many of the conservation initiatives beginning to emerge in the area, particularly the protection of the forest inland and the highly endangered turtle population on the beach.

When Colin first met her she was already in her eighties, but she soon gained a deep appreciation for the work that the A Rocha team and volunteers were doing and for all they stood for. The way that Colin had become part of the community and his intention to stay for the long-haul impressed her a lot. She was a committed churchgoer and the Christian foundations of A Rocha found a genuine resonance with her own beliefs. She knew that her days of running the guest house were very limited so when Colin proposed that it could become an A Rocha centre she immediately welcomed the idea. The financial challenge seemed enormous but her stepson Angus who was by then managing her affairs suggested that it should be rented to begin with and then purchased when that became possible. The location had already proved itself ideal for research and conservation work and an agreement was reached that included provision for Barbara to remain an active participant in the new vocation of the buildings. In the event Barbara died at the age of eighty-seven the day before the team were to move in to join her. Two more nerve-wracking years ensued before sufficient funds were given by a number of friends and supporters so that A Rocha Kenya could secure the property, but now Mwamba – The Rock in Swahili – provides a fine base for the study and protection of this wonderful area.

It was the emerging work in Kenya which first confronted us with the dilemma that has troubled conservation projects from earliest times. It was to become increasingly important to us as more and more A Rocha projects began in countries where the needs of desperately poor local communities threatened the extremely important habitats around them. Scientists from wealthy countries could well be persuaded of the value of these places for the many species that are on the brink of extinction. Arabuko-Sokoke Forest, which together with Mida Creek has been the prime focus for the studies of the Kenyan team, is a classic example of a site which satisfies all the criteria for urgent international protection. As well as the birds I have mentioned (and several others, such as the Sokoke Scops Owl), it holds many globally threatened plants and animals, even if some – like the wonderfully named Golden-rumped Elephant Shrew – spend little time in the media spotlight. This fragment of remaining coastal forest is truly important.

It now comprises a narrow strip only forty kilometres long, a tiny remnant of an East African coastal forest which used to extend for 1,000 times that length from Somalia in the north to Mozambique in the south. Frequently very dry, with an unusually sharp divide between the different species found on the two soils that support the forest, dramatic red earth in one half and pure white sand in the other, it is a place of incredible beauty. Within its shrinking boundaries is found an almost unimaginable diversity of life and it is clear enough to scientists that if the forest were to be lost, a whole treasure-house of species would disappear too.

But for all that, the urgent issues for the families who were living around the forest were ones of survival, of how to secure even the most basic necessities of life. So from their perspective and those of organisations focused on human development issues it made far more sense to attend to the questions of poverty first and only later to begin to consider the apparently secondary interest of securing the forest and its wildlife.

From the very beginning, the Kenyan team included local people who worked alongside volunteers and visitors from wealthier places and together they began to wrestle with these challenges. Because they came from the communities living around the forest, the work they were doing slowly began to have an impact on those villages, schools and churches. As that happened, a number of things became clear.

They saw that underlying many of the arguments lay a kind of conflict model that set the needs of 'the environment' against the needs of 'the people'. The disagreement had become increasingly sharp in development and environmental circles, not least driven by a scramble for donors' attention and funding. All too often there was a tendency for different groups to claim territory or high ground for one priority over the other. But the A Rocha studies were showing how closely related the forest was to the well-being of the creek that supported local fishing, to the local climate that was essential to the crops being grown, to the soils on which the planting was done. Even more, the team's Christian inspiration, their reading of the Bible that was guiding and motivating them, served only to show how it was all inter-connected in God's wisdom and there was no conflict at all between all the different imperatives. However counter-intuitive, it seemed that human prosperity went hand in hand with the well-being of the wider creation.

As the A Rocha team worked with local pastors who were beginning to come to the centre for discussions and explored with them the way that the Bible spoke directly to specific local realities, everyone involved began to understand that it was human rebellion against God that always resulted in environmental degradation and that it wasn't a natural consequence of rightly working the land. Equally, people were seen to flourish in so far as they sought to be a blessing for the whole creation and not merely for human society. The vision of the Old Testament prophets (who were working in an environment threatened in very similar ways to those familiar to rural Kenyan pastors) was that God had created the world for blessing, and their concept of shalom was intended to inspire a truly sustainable environment.

One morning Colin Jackson led a bird-ringing and teaching session which allowed everyone to see and touch local birds. This especially delighted one pastor who admitted to having eaten most of these species. 'But never again!' he declared. 'After this workshop I have changed completely!' Slowly, the local leaders in the community, who were often pastors or the teachers from schools where

A Rocha was working, began to see that it was incoherent for even the poorest Christian community to believe that only by driving other parts of creation to extinction could they survive or develop. Such an over-simplification could only lead to catastrophe for all concerned, as was becoming apparent a few miles to the north where the loss of the Dakatcha forest was already causing desertification and widespread hunger.

It was a really well-designed project that finally put such a powerful vision into local practice. The area had already witnessed a number of well-meaning attempts to alleviate human poverty that had taken little account of local environmental conditions and constraints. At times they had ended by making the situation worse and not better. Colin himself had witnessed a particularly notable example in northern Kenya where boreholes had been sunk for a nomadic people in order to provide a more regular supply of water. Very quickly, the surrounding area had been devastated as people settled down with their livestock and remained nearby for many weeks longer than the arid habitats could support.

After a long process of consultation, the team felt they were finally beginning to understand what was driving the destruction of the forest. Drawing on the hard-won trust of their local friends they became aware that most of the wood was being cut to fund secondary school fees. Only one out of ten children who gained the grades to continue from free primary schooling to secondary education was able to do so, as the modest fees required to continue were out of reach for nearly all. However everyone knew that education was the only way for any family to find its way out of poverty. Proscriptive solutions that simply policed the forest, or educational programmes that extolled the undoubted global importance of its habitats, were never going to make much difference. Neither could take account of the primary needs of the communities which lived around, and so inevitably from, the forest itself.

In order to work towards satisfying all those various urgent needs that the discussions had identified, the A Rocha team began a programme called ASSETS, the Arabuko-Sokoke Schools and Eco-Tourism Scheme. The idea was simple. The programme trained local guides to work with the Watamu hotels so that tourists could visit the forest for a small fee. The United Nations Development Programme and other agencies provided start-up funds for a tree-hide and a spectacular walkway out through the mangroves at Mida Creek for which visitors paid a fee to ASSETS. People began to take advantage of the chance to see such amazing places, and the resultant revenue was then directed to providing secondary school fees for local children. Instead of the forest and creek serving merely as a rapidly diminishing cash fund they became the basis of an income-generating business that could provide school fees for the communities around them.

At the time of writing over a hundred and seventy children are in secondary school and an extensive re-forestry and education programme is going on in many of the villages around the forest. To visit them, as we did last month, is a revelation, and there was no doubting the force of their own conviction that the forest must remain in a healthy state. People have understood that Mida Creek critically requires the secure rainwater supply that percolates down from the forest on its eastern edge. The creek's mangrove fringes in the intertidal zone, once cut for wood, are now secure in their role as nurseries for the fish species on which local people depend for protein. In their minds, and now in ours, it all holds together. In their minds and in ours, God intended it that way.

All of it served to show how giving proper weight to developing deep local relationships and involvement is vital, even to a project like ASSETS. Without careful recognition of all the connections – social, spiritual, environmental and developmental – little progress would have been made. At a superficial level there might seem to be no connection between school fees and the fate of the Sokoke Scops owl, but it proved to be there in the most fundamental ways.

Over the years we have become convinced of the importance of this incarnational approach to conservation questions. Short-term project funding can help significantly for a limited time, but there is always the risk that the analysis of the problems will be superficial. If people are involved for relatively short periods, their departure and the end of the funding usually means the end of all the project aimed to achieve. Long-term work that grows out of what communities themselves want and can do brings its own huge challenges – in particular, the early demands of becoming truly established, both socially and financially, are considerable – but we are persuaded that there are huge relational benefits that more than justify the effort.

Miranda and I were beginning to pack ever more lessons in our travelling bags, a rapidly growing bank of costly experience from a new generation of A Rocha leaders like Colin. Part of our job in coming years was to do all we could to enable them to be widely shared.

Shortly after leaving Kenya at the end of our first trip to Watamu, we were due to visit the small team that we had first got to know in the Bekaa Valley of Lebanon during the travelling year of 1996, whose story I shall tell in the next chapter. We wondered how much of the Kenyan experience would encourage people in such a different place. There would be programmatic ideas to share of course, but most of all we were carrying with us a growing confidence that God truly cared for his own creation. It would be the wisdom of his ways, truly universal in all the diversity of different places, which would keep us all going through the most difficult of times. Through its long and tumultuous history until the very present day, Lebanon tends to specialise in times like those, so that confidence made a good travelling companion as we journeyed on.

Chapter Five:

Beirut, the Bekaa and Beyond

The skeleton of a huge iron steamer, bottom upwards and rent in twain on a rock in front of our bows, appeared strangely out of keeping with the calm beauty of all else around. Like the upturned and contorted strata which underlie the rich and peaceful glades of the Lebanon, it seemed at once an unheeded record of the past and prophecy of the future.[1]

Canon H.B. Tristram, ornithologist, on his arrival in 1863.

'If you think you are beginning to understand this place, then you haven't been properly briefed.'

In the invigorating company of Beirut geology lecturer Chris Walley, we were rattling over the mountains that separate the coastal strip of Lebanon from the Bekaa Valley when he produced this famous UN dictum to encourage us. Leaning out of the window of his old Renault at the frequent check-points to greet the baffling variety of military and para-military groups with what we (and perhaps they) felt was unnecessary high humour, he was clearly doing his best to prepare us for our first encounter with the glory, despair and sheer hard grind of the next A Rocha national incarnation.

Subsequent events have shown his comment to be entirely apt, even allowing for his notorious relish for the apparently impossible. That and his penchant for black humour were doubtless born out of the very tenacious faith which had kept him and his wife Alison in Beirut through some very testing years: perhaps each of us is improbably granted the God-given kit to keep us faithful to our callings? Either way, as we entered our second autumn of travels, we were glad to be introduced to the battered landscapes of this paradoxical country by such an incorrigible enthusiast.

On our whistle-stop tour with Chris we encountered the chaos of the cities, the country's last wetlands and the fragments of cedar forests that still clung on to the steeper mountain slopes. There was clearly a massive challenge ahead if A Rocha were to join with other Lebanese groups to change prevailing attitudes of indifference. Nearly all of the habitats we saw were already severely degraded or in urgent need of some measure of protection, and apparently there were relatively few qualified people remaining in the country who were available to help. Even against the background of the years of civil war that had ended just six years before, in 1990, no one in the fledgling A Rocha team had any idea of the depth of commitment that would be needed to see them over the very first hurdles.

As with many of the early A Rocha projects, the initial effort was built around friendships, and they would sustain all involved through some tense times.

Chris and Alison Walley had come to know of A Rocha through Alison's brother, Simon Marsh, who married our dear colleague Penny Jones following a series of (decreasingly ornithological) visits to Cruzinha in the nineties. For many years the Walleys had lived and worked in Beirut, and during field trips to the Bekaa Valley they had got to know a couple of British teachers, Chris and Susanna Naylor. They were supporting the work of local schools there but were battling with a growing sense of frustration and futility at how little difference they could make to the institutionalised problems of school life in the Bekaa.

Before going further I need to warn you of one of the narrative problems that I face in chronicling many of the national teams – Christian names seem to run in series like London buses: when they appear at all, they arrive in fleets. So just as two of the key people at the outset of the work in Lebanon were both confusingly called Chris, so it is rare to find anyone involved in A Rocha Czech who is not called Pavel, and the name Oscar has a virtual monopoly over the leaders in Peru. Hence our relief when the inimitably named Markku emerged as team leader in Canada. We felt that an apparently superfluous letter was a small price to pay for such welcome uniqueness. Even so, we resigned ourselves to a trend when Tiina was appointed as their administrator. We could only sigh when A Rocha UK recruited another Peter Harris for their team. We see quite a bit of each other's email. I am always being summoned to meetings in west London and he must despair of the random places in the world where he is expected to be with little warning.

To return to Lebanon, the Walley tour had finally brought us to Chris and Susanna Naylor's apartment at the top of the hill in the village of Qabb Elias. From their flat roof, they pointed out the Aammiq wetland just to the south and described how over the past year they had seen it shrinking almost by the day. Chris had been visiting it with increasing frequency and knew it to be the most significant wetland in the country. However, he explained to us that when he tried to understand the causes of its demise, he found that that there is really no such thing as a straightforward answer in Lebanon.

'Any apparently innocent request can often be seen to conceal more complicated issues. "Who wants to know? Why should they?" And people wonder before answering, "What will you do when you know, and who might gain by knowing it?"'

We began to grasp that it didn't take a course in quantum physics, but merely a brief visit to Lebanon, to understand that time and space are not linear. It was also enough to see that the environmental consequences of such a troubled history were as tragic as all the others.

We went to bed at the end of our first evening in the village with our heads spinning. As we lay awake listening to the unfamiliar sound of shelling, far to the south around the border, we wondered if this time the difficulties of the place would prove too great for A Rocha to bring any hope at all. But as soon as we went down to the marsh at dawn the next morning, we knew why everyone there felt that they had to try.

The Aammiq wetland lies at the end of a very narrow corridor that forms an extension of Africa's Rift Valley, directly in the major migration route for hundreds of bird species. Each spring and autumn, millions of birds of prey, storks, wildfowl and waders make their way along the valley between their wintering quarters in Africa and the breeding grounds of Europe and western Asia. The disappearance of the marsh would mean the loss of a vital rung in the ladder of habitats that sustain all these migrants, as well as being a huge blow for a region where water issues have frequently been a major source of conflict. The marsh is also spectacularly beautiful, as it glistens at the foot of the hills, an inviting avenue of trees stretching out from its western edge, remaining green months after the surrounding land has become dusty and parched in the heat of summer.

After we returned to Chris and Susanna's apartment we began to talk. A series of possibilities for A Rocha's work emerged almost abruptly in the conversation, seeming, at that point, nearly as remote as the pale slopes of Mount Hermon gleaming on the southern horizon. Schoolchildren could come over from Beirut to visit – until now all the learning was done in the classroom. University students needed places within the country to do their fieldwork – the more gifted ones seemed always to go abroad at any opportunity. Any wetland site presents multiple possibilities for interesting studies, and how about eco-tourism? It could be a far better use of the marsh than draining it for crops that no longer made economic sense and it could create much-needed employment too. Surely, however, the delicate security situation and complicated logistics would pose almost insuperable difficulties? The questions seemed endless but, as those who work in Lebanon must be, our hosts seemed undeterred. Before we left, we agreed that they would get started as soon as possible on discussions with their current employers and then, if the way ahead opened, embark on the long process of research and consensus-0building that would be needed to lay good foundations for a project.

The months that followed would involve them in fieldwork, lengthy consultations and partnership discussions, not only in the immediate area but throughout the country. Chris and Alison Walley helped to set up a series of meetings in Beirut and it was soon decided that the emerging A Rocha group would try to bring Christian leaders together to consider the case for what would be an entirely new kind of activity for the Lebanese church. Even before a project could get involved with government agencies or other non-governmental organisations (and in Lebanon all had their own official or de facto faith allegiances), an A Rocha team would need to know that there was agreement within their own Christian community and that they had the support of its leaders too. Furthermore, those leaders needed to be convinced not merely about what to do but about why it was important for them as Christians to do it. For a group such as that, biblical reasoning would be even more persuasive than arguments about the country's environmental crises.

Respected figures within Lebanon such as Riad Kassis, Colin Chapman and Issa Diaband quickly agreed to be involved in planning a conference that could spell out the vision and give space for as many people as possible to brainstorm about the possibilities for A Rocha activities. An invitation was sent to John Stott, probably the international Christian leader most respected by all. He is also an enthusiastic birder who has given his support to A Rocha from its earliest days, so Chris Naylor deftly slipped the prospect of finding Pallid Harriers at Aammiq into the invitation and John immediately agreed to come to speak in Beirut the following spring. The event proved to be the most comprehensive gathering of evangelical Christian leaders in Lebanon since the beginning of the civil war in 1975 and it opened the way for many important partnerships with schools and churches in the years that followed. Chris and Susanna have told us since that, although it probably happened too early in the story for maximum impact, even so it was an important first step towards building local ownership of the new vision. For the first time the growing team could cherish the hope that environmental action could become increasingly important to Christian communities in the Middle East.

In the months and years that followed, wonderful and creative work ensued almost exactly as Chris and Susanna had hoped but certainly exceeding the expectations of the rest of us. All kinds of people were involved and not least the Naylor kids, Sam, Chloe and Josh. Their family home became the initial base for all the project work – an experience only too familiar to many A Rocha pioneers! As our own children had done years before in Portugal, the Naylor gang offered a welcome and an educated introduction to the area that was uniquely their own to visitors of all ages who often appeared at their door with little warning.

Alain and Karin Boisclair-Joly arrived soon afterwards from Canada to help with schooling for the children and to begin an educational programme for local schools too. But they soon found that they were almost equally needed to support the family with all the complicated logistics of life in the Bekaa. It was no simple task to juggle the needs of an increasing number of visitors while answering urgent calls to meetings in Beirut and handling the constant unpredictability of local events. Not for the first time, people who were ready to pitch in and do whatever was needed made a vital contribution that made the more recognisably environmental work possible.

The many early days that Chris and Susanna spent talking with landowners and local people soon led to a particularly close partnership with the Skaff family who own much of the marsh with its surrounding land and who have a lot of influence both there and nationally. The family not only agreed to support the restoration of acres of wetland, but put some of their farm buildings at the disposal of the fast-developing education programme. Volunteers got to work and, before long, a small visitor centre was set up which has now welcomed thousands of children from all over the country. The centre, like several other key programmes in Lebanon over the last decade, was funded by the MAVA Foundation and, in April 2000, Miranda and I went back to Lebanon with some of their Lausanne board members so they could see at first-hand the results of their support. Three years on from the initial conference in Beirut there was already a great deal to show for all the work that had been done, even if their visit encapsulated all the contradictory elements that were so familiar to Chris and Susanna and the growing local team.

On our first morning back in the Bekaa Valley, we stood together on the hills overlooking the marsh and could already see that the wetlands extended further than previously and, more than that, the reed beds were flourishing again. A ban on hunting in the area had come into force the year before and the clear spring air of the high plain rang with the calls of flocks of migrating waders and songbirds heading north for the summer. It was an astonishing transformation and, in a moment of particular grace, 2,000 storks appeared at eye level in front of us, drifting away out over the valley, spiralling and glinting in the early warmth of the sun. We could see that this initial spectacle alone had convinced our visitors that their faith in the project had been worthwhile. Later over a meal in Aana, the village just south of the marsh where several of the team were now living, we heard an account of all the studies going on and felt a sense of amazement and pride in our new colleagues who had achieved such a lot in a short time.

'It could all change in a moment but if you are going to work here at all, you just have to live with that,' explained Chris.

We all had a vivid illustration shortly afterwards of what he meant. Just after 2 a.m., Israeli jets screamed over the town of Jdita where we were staying, just north of the marsh, and a second later the walls of our rooms shook as their bombs landed on a small Palestinian camp a mile down the road. Shouting and screaming broke out in the streets below and we wondered how our friends from Switzerland were coping with slightly different conditions from the ones they were more used to; our own sang was a long way from being froid. Talk over the breakfast table was a little muted. Our guests had seen how fragile the prospects for continuing the work would always be but, as they rejoined the team later in the morning, it was equally clear to them that no one there was about to give up easily, despite the ongoing stress. Eight years on from that first visit, MAVA is still supporting the work in Lebanon, so it seems they too were ready to persevere.

Until the 2006 war which brought so much suffering to the country, the work went ahead strongly. Thankfully, as I write, it has again been regaining momentum, although it is uncertain when the next crisis might cause it all to come to an abrupt halt. But over the first eight years there were a series of landmark achievements. The Aammiq wetland itself gained formal protection and is now internationally recognised as a landmark nature reserve and Important Bird Area (IBA), despite the major problems associated with such enterprises on privately owned land. Its area is considerably greater and the habitats themselves are in much better shape. Many researchers have built up a greatly increased understanding of the local ecology, and their work has also led to surveys of other important sites around the country which are now identified for conservation. A series of comprehensive reports on mammals, birds and butterflies appeared, beautifully illustrated by a number of artists who became a part of the team at Aana – Lodi Bernhard, Cheryl Cousins and Laurel Sprenger who, with their husbands, formed the core of the resident team in the village for several years.

I discovered first-hand some of the difficulties that Andy Sprenger and others encountered in their fieldwork when we spent time counting migrating raptors together. We had only just arrived at his chosen vantage point over-looking Lake Qaroun to the south of the wetland when (in an uncomfortable reminder of Colin Jackson's experiences at Alvor) there were shouts from the track below and the sound of weapons being loaded. A dozen Lebanese troops suddenly appeared, leaping out of their jeeps and pouring up the hill towards us. Once again it all ended amicably, this time because their commander had spent some years studying just a few miles away from where Miranda and I were living in France. His happy recollections of student escapades served to defuse the situation, but the episode hardly lent itself to the calm collection of data.

At the flood tide of the team's numbers, before the out-break of the Iraq War in 2003, there were nine people from six countries working on different parts of the project's activities. Some stayed longer than others but many of them took all they experienced in Lebanon with them as inspiration for other projects. Chris and Susanna have experienced very directly the difficulties of remaining long-term but many of those who were part of the work for a shorter time went on to play important roles in emerging projects elsewhere, as Andy and Laurel did on their return to the USA, or as the hydrologist Richard Storey did once back in New Zealand. In turn (and here we risk swerving into a catalogue of Colins that could rival the list of Chris's involved), several ornithologists were drawn from other national projects to provide much-needed skills which, among other things, led to the re-establishment of the national ringing scheme. So I will stay with surnames to salute you, Beale and Conroy!

Again, none of it would have been possible without pro-found relationships and many early friendships had led to direct involvement with the project. Riad Kassis undertook to chair the national committee, fulfilling the hopes of the Walleys that by the time they left the country in 1998 a strong national committee would be in place. Riad brought a long experience of work in the Bekaa Valley through the activities of the orphanage he directed just to the south of the marsh, and he also brought a deep commitment to a creation-founded and Christ-like life and theology, not just to the Lebanon A Rocha but to the wider family of leaders that was developing around the world. The example and influence of what has been done at Aammiq has spread to other sites also and remains a bright and shining light in a troubled part of the world. The ongoing nature of all those troubles (even as I write another car bomb has just gone off in Beirut, seriously damaging the church building where another of our committee members, Joy Mallouh, works as pastor) means that it is impossible to predict what will happen even a week from now.

In Beirut, insecurity and bombings have at times been the norm rather than the exception, and on several occasions the Naylors themselves have been only too close to the explosions. Their gratitude for all the positive achievements is matched by a very sober realism after a decade of false dawns and deep frustrations. Life for the Lebanese team has often seemed a roller-coaster of unpredictable and volatile intensity and yet, more than any other quality, they have required unshiftable persistence. It is only sheer endurance through the years of steady application that has taken any of their projects forward.

Their experience has demonstrated perhaps more vividly than any other A Rocha project that only when people are motivated by deep convictions and heartfelt belief will they have the resources to undertake truly transformative work for nature conservation.

Chapter Six:

The Heart of the Question

Buckland learnedly suggested something about snails which he discovered at the bottom of some extensive limestone borings near Boulogne. This led to a learned disquisition on snails, as to how they bored & where they bored & why they bored & whether they really bored or no. Thought I, if they don't, I don't know who does.[1]

Barclay Fox

We returned from our first visit to Lebanon, as we have always done on subsequent occasions, more than thought-ful. There was a great deal at stake for our new colleagues there and elsewhere. We realised how essential it was that we all understood the distinctives of a Christian approach to conservation challenges.

When we were working in Portugal, we had faced some very practical dilemmas and difficulties and had learned some hard lessons. We were grateful for our years in the complex local situation of Alvor when we had tried to understand what could work both for the good of the area and for everyone involved. But as we spent time with new

A Rocha people in each of the emerging projects the really urgent questions appeared to be quite different. If in Kenya it was acute poverty that threatened even the most important habitats and sites, in Lebanon, after the civil war, it was sudden prosperity and uncontrolled development that was leading to widespread environmental degradation.

There were few precedents for practical Christian initiatives in nature conservation in any of the countries we were visiting, although many churches were now hoping to make a distinctive contribution. Despite their varied circumstances, they all seemed to believe that only a radical transformation could make much local difference. But what would make that possible?

This was the question we faced everywhere, although it went deeper than the contours of each new situation we were encountering as we travelled. As we grappled with the issues together and searched for some answers, a consensus began to appear and slowly we gained a clearer idea of the heart of A Rocha's approach.

The conference in Beirut had shown us the great value of spending time with the Christian community. We had been able to see how the task of caring for creation might come to be understood as a normal expression of a worshipping relationship with God. At the same time, we could see how important it was that those who contributed to the work of the new projects were from a variety of backgrounds and that they might come from groups who had never previously considered environmental questions.

So, as our long-suffering laptop continued to field enquiries about how to begin A Rocha work in new countries, we usually replied by suggesting that the first thing to do was to organise a conference. This went against our activist instincts but we began to see that bringing people together to try to agree that nature conservation was a proper concern for Christians and then to plan some practical activity was the best way to launch an A Rocha initiative. Even the challenge of putting on an event helped the emerging groups to see what capacity they had for any future work and it helped us to understand the different issues that this new concern for nature conservation raised for the churches.

The early conferences drew in business people, nature reserve managers, scientists and theologians, activists and office-bound policy makers. Questions that arose for the Dutch would never occur to Kenyans; North Americans brought a series of perspectives all of their own. Not only were there differences in Christian emphasis, there were conservation priorities which stemmed from choices that were deeply cultural. There was no shortage of paradoxes, either. In the UK, where we were spending time between trips, we could see that the country was increasingly given over to creating wealth in ways that sat uneasily with the particularly British sensibility for 'nature'. But we were not surprised to discover that behind all the differences of approach, whether we were talking with Christian or secular groups, lay our original questions. What would sustain Christian work in conservation and how could it be truly transformative?

As we tried to find the honest answers, we could see that understanding all the different national perspectives would be vital if A Rocha was to find new ways forward and avoid becoming a sterile mono-cultural franchise with an outlook on the world that would remain invariably Western.

Each conference took us a few steps further. An exchange during one of the most recent events showed with particular clarity how national perspectives differ but also the essential commitments that have shaped them all.

In February 2006 we had brought a group of environmental leaders to speak at a conference at Regent College, a graduate theological school in Vancouver, Canada. The aim of the event was to equip people for environmental work in the context of widespread global poverty.

Regent is particularly concerned that Christians from around the world should be able to make an authentic contribution in wider society, so it has always been a very supportive partner for us. All of those speaking on this occasion were Christians, drawn from a number of different cultures and countries. One of the contributors whose words had the most impact was Stella Simiyu: her years working in plant conservation around the world have given her a great deal of experience of the good and the bad in global environmental projects. She had also been involved with A Rocha Kenya from its earliest days and now gives time to A Rocha as an international trustee. In short, she is a gift of God to any environmental organisation but particularly to ours.

After her presentation, she began to field questions. One came immediately from a post-grad student who had clearly thought long and hard about his own life and, as is normal at Regent, wasn't just interested in theory.

'Why don't more of us simply eat the things that are grown locally and in season? How can we possibly defend all the energy use involved in bringing peas from Kenya or grapes from Chile?'

Stella's answer was unexpected in eco-cool Vancouver.

'You just have to consider that poor communities in Kenya have no other markets for their goods, no other way of gaining foreign currency. In Africa, biological diversity has been esteemed by environmental conservationists with a total neglect of the needs of the people – while Christians have only concentrated on the resource value of biodiversity and have neglected conservation. As the Brundtland Report showed, solving our environmental problems requires healthy industries and a healthy economy, simply because it is when an economy is growing that we can afford to make the choices that are essential if we are to live within the planet's means. So if we turn the trading tap off, it will be a catastrophe.'[2]

Stella is constantly seeing the connections – between the well-being of communities in one part of the world and people's way of life in another, between securing the planet's biodiversity but also its inevitable association with justice and food security. She has been one of the A Rocha leaders who have taught us that human communities can only flourish if they are able to live in a way that sustains their surrounding environments. Her Kenyan experience, from the unfortunate 'people versus nature' early experiments in national parks where people were displaced so that large mammals could live undisturbed, to the community resource management plans of more recent times, lay behind her warning: 'As Christians, we cannot afford not to invest in environmental conservation, because this is how we enhance the ability of the rural poor to have options and find ways of getting out of the poverty trap.'

For Stella, as for many of those from countries where the possibility of starvation is a daily reality for millions of people, conservation matters for very different reasons from those that appeal to a Canadian or a European. But the rest of her answer, given as a Christian, took us to the source of the transformation that she believes could make possible a more sustainable way of living on the earth.

'It is the human heart that needs changing,' she said. 'Genuine and lasting solutions from a Christian perspective can only arise out of a foundation of rock, not sand, hence a true and sincere worship. The Bible admonishes us to worship God in spirit and truth, not to ignore the poor, but rather to pursue justice and righteousness. The interconnectedness between people, poverty, environmental conservation, economic growth and sustainable development has been recognised by the mainstream conservation sector. So what are the implications for Christian mission?'

It seemed to those of us who heard her that day that we needed to listen to each other's perspectives more carefully than ever.

In Western society at the beginning of the twenty-first century, all kinds of beliefs are abroad, both expressed and unexpressed, although in the conservation world at least, they are rarely articulated. Tremendous technical competence and a wealth of analytical and material resources are available in what Stella termed 'the mainstream conservation sector'. Even so, it seems that a lack of any compelling motivation to change the way we live is robbing this global effort of much of its effect. Kenyans are able to raise questions about that with far greater confidence and freedom than those of us from the secular West.

Over recent years, comprehensive international studies on biodiversity have been painstakingly compiled by many different organisations. Happily, A Rocha teams are now able to make their own contribution to the essential task of documenting what is happening around the world. All the studies show that a widespread extinction of species is taking place[3] but it seems that we are well able to ignore information which poses an inconvenient challenge to the way we have become accustomed to living, even if we know it can only be sustained at the expense of both the poor and the planet.

The hope that education in itself would be sufficient to bring about change was part of a nineteenth-century developmental myth that should have lost its grip on our imaginations long ago. Yet, because education and legislation are the principal levers of a secular society, they remain centre stage on the platform of environmental campaigning. There is now no shortage of solid science and no lack of research consensus about the environmental crisis which is overtaking the earth that Christians believe to be the very handiwork of a loving Creator.[4] The problem is that when we require information alone to be transformational, we are asking too much of it.

So while it may seem paradoxical for a quintessentially activist organisation like A Rocha to give time and resources to the task of theology, in reality all of us live according to what we believe, regardless of our faith or lack of it. The challenge for Christians is to live by our faith as intentionally as possible. We find coherence and integrity no easier than others; the true consequences of Christian believing are demanding to say the least, which is probably why Jesus tended to speak of them in terms of dying and new life. So to the degree that our relationship with creation either follows or ignores our faith in the God who made it all, we will be agents either of its renewal or destruction. This will be as true in the details of daily living as in the more significant choices that we may be able to make if we live in the wealthier world.

As the rapidly multiplying A Rocha teams continued to craft a workable Christian approach to conservation, we tried to bring our faith to bear at every point, from the minutia of everyday tasks to the big visions that were their justification. Above all, we began to believe that to care for creation was to share the concerns of God himself. It was obvious that the time when churches in wealthy countries could simply baptise unsustainable lifestyles as being some kind of blessing from God were well and truly over. But we were only just beginning to understand why change would be so hard for us all.

The root of the difficulties seems to lie in what now passes for gospel in many parts of the world. It is as if the DNA of Western society has found its way so comprehensively into the authentically Christian original that we have come to believe a genetically modified (GM) version. The driver of this GM gospel is our own self-realisation, whether it is given a 'spiritual' spin (you need Christ to find peace in your life) or is based on the blatantly materialistic promises that originated in the USA but are now heard in the churches that preach the Christian right to prosperity around the world, from Brazil to Nigeria, Korea to South Africa.

Naturally enough, if 'me and my life' is all that the gospel is about, it will do little for the wider creation or even human society and its relationships. When the significance of Christ's death and resurrection for our personal lives becomes the exclusive focus of Christian attention, then we have come a long way from the universal scope of what Jesus called 'the kingdom of God'. A GM church will, however, serve very conveniently for the preoccupations of people in increasingly materialistic and individualistic societies, whether they are rich or poor.

But such a limited view of Christian good news robs the gospel of its transformative power even for people, just as certainly as it eliminates its significance for the rest of creation. The gospel, as the apostle Paul wrote, has 'the glory of Christ'[5] at its heart. It confronts us, as it did those who encountered Jesus when he walked the earth, with the question 'Who is this?', rather than asking 'What do I need? What do I gain by this for my life?' which are the more typical questions of cultures like our own, profoundly influenced as they are by humanism and the Enlightenment. So even though the core beliefs of the Christian faith and the texts that inform them are before our eyes, we simply haven't appropriated them in a way that does them justice. Either we don't think they are important, or the authentic gospel lays such a sharp axe to the root of the cultural trees which shelter and sustain us that we cannot easily open our lives to its challenge.

Many secular writers have also puzzled over the apparent failure of environmental organisations to carry their point in the most affluent and therefore the most environmentally destructive societies. They too have come to the conclusion that we all suffer from a similar corruption or malaise. Here is Curtis White writing recently in *Orion Magazine*.

> We are willingly part of a world designed for the convenience of what Shakespeare called 'the visible God': money. Rather than taking the risk of challenging the roles money and work play in all of our lives by

actually taking the responsibility for reordering our lives, the most prominent strategy of environmentalists seems to be to 'give back' to nature through the bequests, the annuities, the socially responsible mutual funds advertised in Sierra and proliferating across the environmental movement. Such giving may make us feel better, but it will never be enough. ... Even when we are trying to aid the environment, we are not willing as individuals to leave the system that we know in our heart of hearts is the cause of our problems. We are even further from knowing how to take the collective risk of leaving this system entirely and ordering our societies differently. We are not ready. Not yet, at least.[6]

Christians would say that as Christ takes hold of our lives, he calls us into a profound engagement with his world in all its complicated and messed-up reality. If our calling is to bring hope to the whole world, any continuing creation-blindness in the church will be deeply troubling. It will be even more of an anomaly for those of us in the Christian community who claim to recognise biblical authority for what we undertake, because it is Scripture itself that brings creation into the story of redemption.

Gordon Fee is a leading scholar of Paul's writings, and a good friend to A Rocha. He gives an account of research that reviewed a hundred sermons on Romans chapter 8, one of the great Christian doctrinal texts. Disturbingly, only two of them made any attempt to look directly at what it teaches about the redemption of creation.[7] He concluded that we have valued the text for its promise of hope for humanity, but we have missed the significance of its message of hope for the rest of creation.

Furthermore, just as this hope in humanity's future redemption finds practical expression now, so we are called to express that same hope for creation in work for its restoration. We are called to both as signs, in our own times, of God's coming kingdom and final redemption of all things.

Our humanistic bias is equally problematic for ecologically literate critics of Christian belief who have concluded, perhaps quite reasonably, that our faith seems irrelevant to the world they live in. John Stott has expressed the problem with his usual crisp logic. 'We evangelicals have tended to have a good doctrine of redemption and a bad doctrine of creation. Of course we have paid lip-service to the truth that God is the Creator of all things, but we seem to have been blind to its implications.'[8]

In recent decades, not least as a result of John Stott's influence, a huge sea change has taken place in evangelical thinking. Even during the two years during which I have been writing this book, its pace has been accelerating to the point where the *New York Times* has been only one of many papers to take notice.[9] It has been heartening to see creation-friendly ideas being articulated for the first time by quite conservative evangelical leaders. It takes courage to say, as Duane Litfin, President of Wheaton College, Illinois did when talking to the same newspaper in February 2006: 'The evangelical community is quite capable of having some blind spots, and my take is that climate change has fallen into that category.' In 2006 he was one of eighty-six evangelical leaders in the United States who put their name to a call for action saying, 'millions of people could die in this century because of climate change, most of them our poorest global neighbours'.

However, even if the journey back to a more biblical base for these issues has been well begun, we must be sure

to follow it to the end. It is entirely reasonable and emi-
nently pragmatic to appeal to human suffering as our reason for not abusing the creation, but that is only part of the
biblical imperative. If our central argument is that people
will suffer if we don't care for creation, we are still thinking more like humanists than Christians. 'Human well-
being is what really matters' is the unconscious sub-text of
this version of environmental theology. The full scope of
the Christian gospel extends much further, even if our own
salvation is the starting point and even if it is our transformation in Christ that gives hope for the earth itself.

The search for human well-being at any cost has always
been an inadequate criterion for environmental decision-
making. It is that kind of reductionist logic that has
already led us to make a desert of large areas of God's good
earth. We need a better motivation than a concern for our
own well-being, or even for the well-being of the poor, if we
are to truly change the way we treat the creation around
us. Industrial societies now face acute difficulties as they
try to translate the conclusions of climate change science
into policies that are acceptable to the electorate. It
appears that there is a yawning gulf between our environmental rhetoric and the choices we are prepared to make
in practice.

Lt General Roméo Dallaire was the Force Commander
of the United Nations Assistance Mission for Rwanda
(UNAMIR) at the time of the 1994 genocide. His searing
reflections on what he has called 'the failure of humanity'
make telling reading if they are transposed from the
humanitarian context to the environmental.

We have fallen back on the yardstick of national
self-interest to measure which portions of the planet we

allow ourselves to be concerned about... Are there any signs that we are prepared to take the higher road in international human relations? Not many... In the last decades of the twentieth century, self-interest, sovereignty, and taking care of number one have become the primary criteria for any serious provision of resources or support to the world's trouble spots.[10]

Stella Simiyu has been one of many to demonstrate how environmental degradation and climate change hurt poor people the most. It is in the poorer communities of the south that the most grievous impact is felt, yet the wealthier societies whose emissions are causing the problem may even benefit by higher temperatures and the other short-term changes taking place. It will be counter-intuitive for societies that retain their own well-being at heart to change their ways unless they are given more fundamental reasons for doing so than enlightened self-interest.

Of course, a concern for the poor and for straightforward justice are sufficient reason for us to change. But the transformation that will enable both to endure can only come from a renewed relationship with the Creator. Only life in Christ will release us all, rich or poor, from seeing creation as merely raw material to meet our human needs. The care of creation, like compassion for people, is the true consequence of knowing that we share a loving Creator. But to make people's needs the justification for environmental concern is to establish a dangerous hierarchy that leaves us, and not God, in pride of place. We care for God's creation because he does and because we live in his ways, not just because we need it.

So we can hope that a rediscovered evangelical compassion for suffering humanity will lead us to respond to the suffering of creation itself. Paul, in the neglected

105

Romans 8 passage, talks of the 'groaning' of creation and it is that groaning which urgently needs to reach our newly attentive ears. If we risk losing an unprecedented range of flora and fauna in the coming years through human negligence or greed, those who believe that these species and their habitats are God's handiwork cannot remain indifferent. But it will be our renewed relationship to God the Creator that will inspire us to live rightly with his creation.

These were the convictions that were beginning to form the common thinking of all those now becoming involved in A Rocha around the world. As we rehearsed them in many different places, we found ourselves engaging in a kind of environmental education that was going to be an important element of A Rocha's future work.

Miranda and I knew that we had been given a gift of time to develop A Rocha's ideas in company with many others, and we had been asked by the Trustees to make some continuing international work a part of our future role. But as the winter of 1996 began, we had been living out of suitcases for a year and a half and were beginning to feel the need to put down some roots somewhere. We were also longing to create a single focus for our activities and it would be a relief from the intensity of the previous months to be able to think about working on a field project again.

As we considered where all of these hopes might take a local form, we turned our eyes towards France.

Chapter Seven:

The French Exception

The French are a logical people, which is one reason the English dislike them so intensely. The other is that they own France, a country which we have always judged to be much too good for them.[1]

Robert Morley

We had retained hopes of working in France since the earliest days of our marriage. Simple convictions lay behind the idea, as they had behind the choice of Portugal for the first A Rocha project. Why live in a country where there are already good numbers of other Christians and why do conservation in a place where many others are already active?

Perhaps a certain realism was also creeping in with our older years. Wouldn't it be pleasant to work in a language we already knew? Miranda had been a French teacher and had spent two years living in St Etienne and Dijon. Even my own rather haphazard exposure to the language – culminating in random and over-sophisticated Cambridge afternoons reading Verlaine and Rimbaud with the exotic Madame Grillet – had left me enough of a shaky foundation to build on. It was, of course, an entirely useless preparation for anything remotely practical such as replacing a tyre, or dealing with the sequellae of that national treasure and heritage, rural plumbing. A student job in an Issoire car factory had laid down a more effective vocabulary for anything like that, even if the majority of the expressions were unsuitable for polite company. If we were to move to France, it was clear that my initial efforts in the language would swerve between the pompous and the profane, ideal for striking up friendships and banishing stereotypes about the English.

So, all things considered, the idea of moving to France to begin another A Rocha initiative returned as a wise option at a time when our teenage offspring were all studying in the UK and our parents were getting no younger.

A chapter of *Under the Bright Wings* explains how we understood the process of being in some way guided by God in the early days of deciding whether we should work in Portugal. This time round, the months went by and no clear direction seemed to emerge from all the possibilities. The only conviction we had was that how we lived was of more significance than where we eventually found ourselves, or even what we did when we got there.

In truth, only a very small percentage of people, even in wealthy countries, have much choice in such matters. For most Christians throughout history, the principal question has been how to live the often incomprehensible, uncontrollable and gritty set of circumstances that hold them fast. By contrast, it appeared that we were at the ultra-privileged end of the spectrum where we had almost unlimited choice and with the possibility of doing something governed by the logic of vision. We were grateful but knew we could hardly universalise the experience.

So, accompanied by close friends and praying churches, we accepted that the truly important part of the process was to keep praying and listening, researching and discussing. And, in the absence of any certainties, we should probably just get on and make up our minds.

As a first step we decided to spend a month in France in order to see if a new centre there might be viable. Perhaps I should confess at this point to a perverse English conviction that if an A Rocha project could work in a country not traditionally receptive to initiatives anglo-saxoniques, it could work anywhere.

So in mid November we set off on our own Tour de France in a borrowed car, looking for a suitable area to begin work and eventually to establish a centre. It needed to be easy for students to reach by public transport and there were other requirements that suggested themselves: a nearby local community to which we could all belong and a region where we could contribute something towards conservation. We ourselves needed to be close to an international airport, something which would also be important for visitors; we knew, as we hadn't in Portugal ,that many of the students and volunteers now interested in A Rocha would arrive from outside France. We also had a suspicion that Mediterranean habitats would soon be a programmatic focus as work in Lebanon emerged to complement the long-term studies in Portugal.

There was only one difference from the criteria we had established during the search for a place to begin work in Portugal: we hoped this time round simply to belong to a local church, rather than attempting to start one as we had in Vila Verde. We knew we would be away too often and when we had lived in the Algarve we had never managed to square the circle of the demands of life in an A Rocha centre with the major effort needed to plant a church.

A month of reconnaissance in France in December hardly qualifies as an adventure, although the truckers' strike that cut off fuel supplies throughout the country gave us some interesting moments and stranded us in some unlikely places. We began by establishing a base for our explorations in a borrowed cottage near Bordeaux. It was freezing, so we dragged a mattress into the small front room and slept in front of the fire. But the greatest consolation of that particular site was the spectacle of 2,000 Common Cranes apparently migrating south, high and noisy, into the winter sunset. By the end of the week, we would gladly have followed them to warmer latitudes.

We were nearly at the end of our trip and beginning to despair of finding anywhere that would really work, when we came across the Vallée des Baux.

An introduction to the community of Pomeyrol in the Alpilles, just to the north of the valley, had taken us there. Friends near Aix-en-Provence had told us we were sure to be welcome – and so it proved. The nuns were well-informed, dynamic and deeply prayerful. We soon found out that they could also be challenging company for casually-minded Anglicans like us.

Our stay with these remarkable women began inauspiciously. We were still in our earliest days of emailing, and I persuaded them to allow me to plug my rudimentary laptop into their antiquated phone system. When I dialled the server, all the phone bells around the community houses were triggered. My attempts to reassure the sisters by showing them how messages were arriving from all over the world only served to increase their alarm in the presence of this demonic technology. As I look back, probably half a million messages later (how I wish that were hyperbole), I can see that their suspicions were entirely justified. We should have embarked upon a full-scale exorcism there and then.

Recovering from this early setback over a meal of soup and bread later that evening, we eyed each other somewhat warily until Soeur Danielle, who led the community, broke the silence in which they usually ate.

'So... Monsieur le Pasteur, tell us about yourselves.' Long pause, and then some halting replies from me during which Portuguese continually swamped my half-forgotten French. Thankfully, Miranda's fluency was on hand to carry the discussion forward.

'Well, we heard you care about how Christians work with the land around them. Do you think that a field centre to encourage some specific projects would be welcome in this part of the world?'

To our astonishment, they sketched out a sophisticated eco-theology that would have borne favourable comparison with any of the others we had yet encountered. Deftly weaving insights from Leonardo Boff into conclusions from Jurgen Moltmann, they gave us an account of how they had been putting some of their ideas into practice on the forty acres of woodland which they were stewarding as community land. It was the first of many times that we learned not to underestimate them.

Probably as a result of the enthusiastic way that they were praying, we found an area in the valley that met all the criteria for fieldwork during the week that followed, and soon afterwards we located a place to rent in a nearby village. The team at another Christian centre where we had also stayed, Eau Vive at Ventabren, were equally supportive and offered to help us find a car and some second-hand furniture. So, braving the barrages of the truckers' strike and the fuel shortages, we set off back to the UK with plans to return for good in the New Year.

Knowing where we were going to settle was a relief to us all. The constant moving around had been a logistical challenge for a family of six, and each of us had lived the more difficult moments in his or her own way. We had known a lot of kindness from many people which had made all the explorations possible, and we had certainly needed some time to reflect on the lessons learned in Portugal before going on to a new adventure. Our oldest daughter Jo, who had by then begun a gap year, teaching in rural Zimbabwe, has written very movingly in her book *Through the Dark Woods*[2] about the impact on her own life of that time, with all its uncertainties. Miranda, with her characteristic courage, took on the challenges presented by travelling without a base to return to, but it was far from an easy process. To her journal she had added the lines a friend had passed on:

> *Willingly transplanted,*
> *I still suffered the shock of new soil.*
> *But I have discovered that*
> *Rooted in Christ*
> *I can grow in any place*

Now that we could envisage the luxury of unpacking, we realised that all the moving around had helped us to see more clearly which things really mattered. On our first Sunday back in the UK, we parked the car outside a church that was supporting us. In the back was all that we had taken with us for the year, a carefully calculated ration of one bag each. They held clothes for all climates with enough personal treasures for the family to keep a sense of home in each of the places where we unpacked. Just before we left Cruzinha, our youngest daughter Beth had been given a rather smart bag and so, when the car was broken into, hers was the one to go. The church immediately responded with a generous gift and she had the unaccustomed experience of buying new clothes.

In fact Beth's first year after leaving Portugal continued to be a roller-coaster. Following the others down a road we had determined she would never have to take, she began at boarding school as we improvised ways of holding family life together in all the changes of country and work. Just as the first term began, we learned she needed quite serious surgery, but she astonished us all by announcing that she was going to be just fine – it seems to us all she has been fine ever since. Esther and Jeremy lived the transitions with courage and remarkable equilibrium, and it was certainly a help that they were all able to be at the same school. Much of what they have all done since seems to indicate that they aren't particularly rooted in Europe, but perhaps they also found deeper roots for their faith, and a sense of what was important to them. I must remember to ask them next time we are on the same continent.

So, after one final Christmas in another borrowed flat, in February 1997 we moved to a small village near Arles.

In a country which, as de Gaulle pointed out, has 200 cheeses, we probably should not have been surprised that starting an A Rocha project was never going to be straightforward. If there are rules anywhere about how national A Rocha organisations should be established, they were nearly all broken in France. For a start, this was hardly a national initiative in the way that other new A Rocha projects have been since. Even worse, it was arriving by means of the traditional enemy from north of the channel, armed with what could only be perceived by the French as another perfidious idea for the erosion of national genius.

Even people in our closest circle of supporters at home could not hide their reservations. As we announced our final decision to move across the channel, my own father looked at me in pained astonishment before saying firmly, 'But we don't like the French!'

Furthermore, we have always known that the priority lies in building the team rather than securing the facilities, but in France it wasn't to work like that.

As a consequence, we were often well out of our depth. Part of the difficulty was that environmental concerns were a minority interest in France at the time, although this was to change quite rapidly. Equally, there weren't many committed Christians in France of any persuasion and it seemed that their visibility in wider society was quite limited. We soon found that there were very few people with much spare capacity to respond to another bright idea and those who might were already much in demand. It was going to be an uphill struggle to find colleagues or supporters.

So the earliest members of the team came from outside France: Rob and Petra Crofton, British and Dutch respectively and Sarah Walker, a Canadian. Canadians continued to make up the early team members as Alain and Karin Boisclair-Joly had now returned from Lebanon and were keen for another challenge. We really discovered the depth of their commitment to A Rocha when we heard that they had raised their support to work with A Rocha Lebanon by foregoing any wedding presents. It seemed it would be hard to find environmentally enthusiastic Christians in

France with that kind of dedication, but Rob's tireless trekking round all the different conservation and Christian conferences led to our meeting Frédéric Baudin, theologian and ecologist extraordinaire, at exactly the right moment both for him and for us.

Frédéric had a pioneer's readiness to take risks with his personal finances in order to give time to building the organisation. It has to be said that in Elizabeth he has a treasure of a wife well able to cope with the inevitable disappointments that such visionaries usually encounter on a daily basis. It was Frédéric's introductions that led us to the first members of a national committee which took shape under the benevolent and wise leadership of Pierre Berthoud. He and his wife Danièle hosted committee meetings quite unlike any other, however familiar the essential ingredients. Leisurely evening discussions during which our innumerable, intractable problems seemed unable to disturb Pierre's possum-like equilibrium were merely the prelude to a magnificent dinner cooked by Danièle. These masterpieces began around ten at night, finished well after midnight, and were probably only a showcase for a series of bottles, lovingly produced from the Berthoud cellar. If, as occasionally happened, Danièle was away and we were obliged to eat out, Pierre's typical tactics on reviewing the wine list went as follows:

'Well, here is a quite presentable Bordeaux. After all that hard talking we probably wouldn't regret that.' Pause...

'Yes well, par contre, I see that for three euros more we could avoid the regrettable acidity of 2002 and safely go for the 2001.' Pause...

'Of course, having decided that, and perhaps we

shouldn't be precipitate, it does seem a shame not to take advantage of what I observe to be a very fair price for the '99... which, as is clear, could make our meal far more memorable.' Pause...

And so on, until we had all been committed, quite effortlessly, to a week's wages for Pierre's eventual choice.

We discovered the French to be Latins of a different kind to the Portuguese, despite their shared love of good company, long stories, and the sacramental possibilities of the simplest of meals. Compared to the issues that are important to ruthless Anglo-Saxon pragmatists, the important questions for our national colleagues seemed to run along the lines of the parody, 'That's all very well in practice, but how does it work in theory?' My own patent lack of Cartesian rigour was frequently the despair of these most philosophically-minded people. I know a discussion is just beginning to warm up when they shout at me: 'Be lucid!'

The eccentrically imposing buildings that became our field study centre near Arles really tore up the A Rocha rule book of 'people first, then property'. We had been learning, instructed by new friends among the students and faculty of Regent College, to embrace the given context of our lives and the given places. We were trying to spend rather less time dreaming of ideal and easier scenarios where Christian living would be more viable, so, as we prayed and planned for a centre, we looked towards some ordinary and difficult choices. Perhaps we could use some accommodation on the farm in our new study site at Les Marais de L'Ilon? The elderly owners seemed to like our company, needed more help, and were increasingly appreciative of what we were doing there. Or maybe we could rent somewhere until A Rocha France had the capacity to think about buying a place? At our worst and over-dramatic moments, we began to think we should all give up and go home.

As the months passed and none of these approaches to finding a base seemed to be getting us anywhere, we felt we were losing momentum. We were nearing the limits of what we could achieve within the improvised arrangements needed to keep the project alive.

What happened next still causes us all kinds of questions. In the autumn of 1998, I met an elderly British gentleman on a flight from London to Marseille. We had a brief and rather anguished conversation about the appalling sights he had witnessed during the war and how they had made it almost impossible for him to believe there could be a loving God. A few days afterwards I was still troubled by what he had told me, so I dug out his card and posted him a copy of *Under the Bright Wings* with a note offering to continue talking on another occasion.

He never wrote back, but a couple of months later news reached us of a major anonymous donation to A Rocha, larger than any we had ever received. We tried unsuccessfully to find out who it had come from, but one Saturday morning my friend from the plane called to ask if I could visit him in London. 'By the way,' he ended, 'I hope you were glad of my donation? Must have given you a good surprise, hey?'

A few weeks later I duly went to his house for dinner so we could continue our conversation. As I did so, I remembered him telling me that, on a whim, he had once bought a house in France for a friend. His donation showed that he liked the work we were doing, so I decided to ask him if he would like to buy another place which we could then rent or borrow from him to use as a centre. To my astonishment he agreed without a moment's hesitation.

Some weeks of discussions followed between our lawyers and his, during which it transpired that it would suit him better simply to give the money, rather than having another house to worry about.

We went together to see Les Tourades, the only house for sale in the valley that had potential as a field study centre. He liked it immediately, but on his return to London he sent the money to me personally, care of a bank in Carpentras, with instructions that I should collect it in cash and pay the owner straight away. This seemed a poor idea for all kinds of reasons and, to my relief, he eventually agreed to repatriate it all so that the A Rocha office could formally receive the gift. Thankfully, during the week that the funds sat in France, the euro rose strongly against the pound, and he gained a great deal by doing it more calmly within UK charity laws. To the very end of the saga we never quite knew what he would decide to do next; we had some surreal discussions with the increasingly incredulous but intrigued owner as completion date approached. But finally, Les Tourades was ours, even if we were hardly yet equipped to run it as a field study centre. Our benefactor's brisk judgment on the adventure some years later seemed entirely in character. 'The best thing this miserable old man did in his entire life!'

So, well before we had a complete team of committed people with a shared vision and the necessary gifts to make it work, we had acquired a world-class set of buildings ideally suited for all we could have hoped for. In the face of such a major step forward, even if it came in the wrong order, the French committee had put aside some of their reservations and agreed that we could hardly refuse the offer. We decided we would simply work it out as best we could.

We did, through many ups and downs. As I write these pages, A Rocha France is led by the extraordinary Paul Jeanson, Christian adventurer and man of faith sans pareil. Whether it is his past as a driver on the Paris-Dakar rally or the years he spent running his own sizeable family estate that gives him his love for adrenaline we have never decided, but he certainly thrives on doses that would normally kill a horse. The more bleak the news that we bring to team meetings, the more his eyes light up, which makes him remarkably bracing company. Working with him is never dull.

We are also blessed with a really solid team. François and Sophie were another find of Rob's, encountered when he was exploring the wetland sites of the Camargue. They had subsequently gone to work in Madagascar for a couple of years but, on their return, they were ready to work with A Rocha. Their arrival brought a very high level of ability to the field studies together with a deep and, by then, suitably African commitment to community. Frédéric was also looking out for potential team members and, when speaking near Paris, met a young biologist with administrative skills, Priscille Pelletier, who was ready to join us just when we needed to coordinate the growing number of volunteers and visitors who were beginning to arrive. Finally, Jean-Pierre and Martine Charlemagne completed the core of a national team, offering their early retirement years to ensure that both the community and buildings stay in good shape so that the house can run at full capacity. Rob and Petra, Alain and Karin, and all the other long-term volunteers who took on a heroic and resilient relay to get us to this point can know that their work was all worthwhile.

We conclude that the Lord is happy to take risks we

wouldn't consider and don't always understand. I personally conclude that, in trying to give some leadership, I will never get to the mythical point where I am free from making mistakes that will put others at risk. Were it not for the grace of forgiveness and the truth of redemption, I would never go outside my front door.

A former politician who shares our Christian commitments told us categorically, with that particular Gallic grace that we have come to know so well: 'You will never establish A Rocha here – you have heard of the exception française? Anywhere else, maybe, but you have to understand that here religion is religion and public life is public life. It is quite impossible to be simultaneously an environmental and a Christian organisation.' There were times in the early years when it seemed she was right.

The French legal structures demand that as a charity you must choose between being a cultural or a religious organisation. This is a joy for the budding language student, as the choice is between 'culturel' and 'cultuel'. Never has a missing consonant been more discouraging: if you choose to be cultural then you fit under a legal framework established in 1901 and the churches cannot support you. If, on the other hand, you choose to be religious, then you set yourself up as an 'Association 1905', which then means that financial help from the state will be closed to you. As everyone pays such high taxes, there is very little tradition of private philanthropy and a very great expectation that the state will take care of things. These two dates took on a sombre significance for our accounts as we finally opted to go cultural and 1901.

In these particularly technical discussions, Arnaud Monnoyeur was a true companion until his untimely death from cancer in 2005. He had been a fellow student with Frédéric Baudin but had never been persuaded by Christian arguments. Even so, on a personal quest to know more before finally making up his mind, he joined us as treasurer. The first meeting we organised together was a fine illustration of all the paradoxes and complications faced by Christians wishing to be involved in public life in France and made the point with almost comic intensity for both of us. We had decided that the moment had come when we should introduce A Rocha to our local mayor, who, as it happened, was one of the few Communist mayors left in the country and so even more wary of anything that looked like religion in public life. Unsure of the reception we would get, Arnaud and I were ushered into his office at the appointed hour, but he remained bent over his papers in a remarkable breach of normally punctilious French courtesies. Our greetings trailed away and we waited. After what seemed like a full minute he leaned back on his mayoral chair and gazed at us for further long seconds in complete silence, clearly at a loss as to how to place us.

'Alors,' he said, 'you are what precisely? Environmental I know, Christian I know... well, more or less I know it. But Christian environmental, c'est quoi exactement?'

Whether we explained exactement we will never know, but the discussion was certainly interesting. Pierre Berthoud had always felt that regardless of any environmental gains we might make, we might also be part of a long overdue examination of 'laicité'. This subtle and sacred idea insists on the exclusion of belief from civil society but does so on the basis of its own essentially credal affirmation of the very particular tenets of secularism. So, as our conversation with the mayor progressed, it was obvious that our own conviction that environmental choices are necessarily based upon values, which themselves derive from beliefs, made exactly the kind of sense that is persuasive to the deeply logical French mind. We also discovered, as we have often done since, that the exchanges became unexpected at the point when the same questions about belief that Christians grapple with are necessary to conservation discussions on all sides of the table. Our partnerships with other groups inevitably lead us to discover what matters to them; the success of a joint project requires that everyone can explain what their hopes of success might mean. As we do so, a discussion of values, beliefs and commitments are frequently a very helpful, if unfamiliar, part of the conversation.

Spending time with another local research organisation shortly afterwards, we discovered that secularism could be problematic for anyone working in conservation. Their team were holding a day-long meeting at Les Tourades and they invited us to join them at the outset to compare notes. As François introduced a report of the work he was doing, he briefly referred to his frustration that a Christian charity which is not specifically Catholic can often be regarded as a cult or a sect on its first contact with a government office. But I think he was as surprised as all of us by the reaction of the other group's director. 'We feel exactly the same,' he explained. 'Scientists of all beliefs and none seem now to be regarded with an equal suspicion. I wish it wasn't like that, but I have to say we can completely identify with what you are talking about.' Apparently we weren't the only ones to suffer from the lack of a public space where the more fundamental motivations that sustain any research organisation can be acknowledged.

From this encounter and many others that have followed, we have come to understand that even in a rigidly secular society like France, questions of belief matter far more than is generally acknowledged. Studies of the world around us seem inevitably to lead us to considerations well beyond apparently isolated physical phenomena. Even the most rigorous of materialists seem to find it hard to avoid less tangible relationships and connections for long. Questions of economics, justice and community soon impose themselves on what can begin as a simple discussion of biodiversity. As we engaged in an increasing number of exchanges at that level, we were able to see that Christian thinking might help to make those connections work better.

But in order to explain what I mean, we need to look more closely at the inspiration for those ideas in biblical thinking.

Chapter Eight:

Change from the Inside

Howbeit, fasting or feasting, we both know this:
without the Spirit we die.[1]

W.H. Auden

I can remember one sparkling spring morning sitting with the family on the cliffs near Tarifa in the south of Spain. We watched in wonder as thousands of birds of prey passed over our heads in an almost continuous stream, arriving on broad wings across the straits from the African coast, dimly visible to the south. For millennia the continents of Africa and Europe have been joined by the seasonal pilgrimages of these most impressive of birds.

It was only later in the day, as the sky cleared of eagles that we lowered our eyes to take note of a quite different migration passing through the same narrow channel. Just below us the mixed traffic of the maritime world was also making its way through the straits, for better or worse. The ships were carrying all kinds of goods for much-needed trade but others, we knew, would be loaded with toxic waste for disposal on west African shores. Some, perhaps, were transporting arms to fuel Africa's conflicts, lethal cargo that is leading to the collapse of the very ecosystems on which the raptors over our heads depended.

Our world is connected in the most direct ways, but although they are often under our gaze they are all too frequently far from our attention. A Christian approach to conservation begins by making those connections and draws on several foundational biblical passages that we need to consider now. Paul's preaching in Athens[2] is a good place to start because it speaks directly to many of our current challenges.

As our narrative makes space for some biblical reasoning, I am encouraged by the solid black page that Lawrence Stern had printed into his highly original novel, *Tristram Shandy*. For those of my conservation friends who are not themselves Christians, I may seem to be embarking now on explanations that are similarly opaque. If so, I recommend that, like Stern's readers, you move on to pages that are more accessible. However, for those who want to get to the heart of the Christian approach to conservation that has shaped A Rocha's practical projects, this section is going to be essential. And so I end my apologies.

First-century Athens exhibited many of the features of our own times, so it is not surprising that Paul's message can resonate strongly for us. He was talking in a city that was cosmopolitan and pluralist, a novelty-minded cultural crossroads. It lay at the heart of a region where Greek was spoken widely and to which the pax Romana had contributed social stability, so travel was relatively straightforward for the empire's citizens, as it is for us. On a regional scale, the same kind of hegemony existed there which we see more widely now as the consequence of globalisation. As a result, when Paul looked for a hearing for his message he did so among many others seeking the same kind of response, even if his gospel made unique claims.

Perhaps that was why he began by observing that knowledge and ignorance seem to grow in equal measure in a rapidly expanding intellectual universe.[3] We could make the same observation about our own times: the hoped for connection that has been the promise of cheap travel, internet, free telephony and the rapid transfer of information seems to have delivered the phenomenon of distance as effectively as it has facilitated global community.

All the statistics show the rich becoming richer and rarer as the poor become poorer and more plentiful. At the turn of the century David Kilgour, former Canadian Secretary of State for Africa and Latin America, pointed out, 'It is a telling reality that the assets of the world's richest three billionaires exceed the combined GNP of all the least developed countries and their 600 million nationals. The global community has a long way to go when three billion people live on less than \$2 per day.'[4] More recent figures from Bill Rees at the University of British Columbia, Vancouver, suggest that the richest fifty people in the world enjoy a combined income greater than that of the poorest 416 million, and just 25 million rich Americans, or 4 per cent of the world's people, have a combined income greater[5] than that of the poorest 2 billion people – 43 per cent of the world population.

Though we consider ourselves to be well-informed, major diseases such as arsenicosis, which afflicts more people worldwide than are affected by HIV/AIDS, remain largely unreported.[6] The casualties of Africa's wars are numbered in millions, and yet they are rarely in the headlines of the Western world. Events in Angola, Sudan, the Democratic Republic of Congo or Ethiopia, have no impact on our own lives and so simply do not figure in the picture we hold of the world.

These simple examples serve to show that information and mobility alone cannot make the connections which the Christian gospel urges on us. The narrative of our information follows our interests, which all too often are reduced to the merely commercial. Technology, in turn, serves the meaning of the markets, so it is now far more difficult to form relationships that will follow the logic of a truly human set of connections. Those relationships are born when we recognise that we share a common Creator, and that where we live is not merely our environment, but his creation.

In the commercial world, legal and political fictions can make it extremely hard to find out who is responsible for what; questions of responsibility and rights have never been more difficult to determine. When Paul asks us to recognise that because we share a common Creator, we form an indivisible community, he makes his appeal to the human heart, the place of potential transformation. All of us know that those hearts beat everywhere, not least behind the walls of apparently impersonal institutions, but it often takes a crisis to bring the disconnects to light. Among them a failure to understand the link between the environment and the people who live in it can be the most tragic.

This was the burden of the letter Vinoth Ramachandra sent us after the tsunami of December 2005 hit the coast of Sri Lanka. 'It took the arrival of the tsunami on our shores to reveal what many local people had known for years – that the destruction of the coastal mangroves and coral reefs, and the injustice that pushed poorer communities to live on vulnerable coastal lowlands, known to be at risk, could amplify a natural disaster into a human catastrophe on a huge scale.'

The first A Rocha leaders meeting in July 1999 brought together (l to r) Colin Jackson (Kenya), Alain Boisclair-Joly (helping with the meeting en route to Canada from work in Lebanon – Karin Boisclair-Joly was the photographer); Anne & Dave Bookless (UK); Susanna & Chris Naylor (Lebanon); Barbara Mearns (A Rocha Administrator) Fréderic Baudin (France); Matthias Stiefel (Chair of the Trustees); Seated: Peter & Miranda Harris; Jane & Mark Bolton (Portugal), Children: Chloe and Josh Naylor, Jack Bolton, Sam Naylor.

The eighth A Rocha Leaders' Forum (at Watamu in Kenya) in April 2007 brought together delegates from 17 national organisations, several potential new national groups, the International Team and the International Trustees.

Some of the A Rocha Brazil team with the guests at their launch conference in São Paulo in November 2006: Marina Silva, Minister of the Environment and Prof Sir Ghillean Prance (together, centre) and the author (back left).

The growth of A Rocha has made it possible to begin collaborative research and conservation programmes, the first focusing on the *Paeonia*. Some of the Bulgarian team (seen here) are studying the Red Peony in the Konjavska Mts whilst A Rocha Portugal is studying the Western Iberian Peony in the Serra de Monchique.

Local volunteers at the Canada Centre in British Columbia potting seedlings for the native tree nursery.

Will Simonson (Scientific Director) and Pavel Svetlik (A Rocha Czech Director) identifying plants together in 2002.

Markku Kostamo, Lennart Saari and the author in Finland in April 2002.

Les Tourades, the A Rocha centre in Provence, France, March 2004.

Melissa Ong filming part of an A Rocha video in the Ilon Marsh, paddled by François Tron, the A Rocha France Science Officer.

Some of the French team (with volunteers from Canada, Finland, the UK and the Netherlands) hiking in the Alps, summer 2007.

Daryl Bosu and Eric Akuba outside the A Rocha Office in Damongo, northern Ghana, in November 2006.

Ghanaian children in 2007 with some of the first tree seedlings planted by A Rocha's Climate Stewards initiative: www.climatestewards.net

The Indian Star Tortoise is at risk of extinction because it is hunted for food, traditional medicines and the pet trade. Vijay D. Anand, Director of A Rocha India, and a colleague (Surendra Varma) collaborated with the Wildlife Trust of India to investigate the illegal and secretive ways in which it is traded.

Gerry Rawcliffe, an International Trustee and long-term supporter, ringing in the Camargue in 2000.

Children living near A Rocha's field study centre in Kenya planting mangrove trees on World Environment Day, 5 June 2004.

Colin Jackson, the A Rocha Kenya Director, started the Nairobi Ringing Group and has many opportunities for training Kenyans and researchers from across Africa in identification, ringing and research skills.

Jonathan Baya, ASSETS Conservation Officer with A Rocha Kenya, visiting the family of a Nyari Primary School child who gained a place at secondary school thanks to an ASSETS eco-bursary.

The site at Minet in Southall, London, transformed, and hosting a pond-dipping expedition.

The Aammiq Wetland in the 1990s, threatened by total destruction due to drainage for agriculture.

The Aammiq Wetland in 2005 after A Rocha Lebanon began to protect and restore the marshes, working closely with Michel Skaff and his family who are the main landowners.

A Rocha Lebanon and SPNL undertook an ambitious three-year programme to identify the most Important Bird Areas in the country. Here, Rob and Petra Crofton, Marius Teeuw, Richard Prior, Colin Conroy and Erik Koppelaar are counting migrating raptors in April 2005.

A Rocha Netherlands has sent many skilled volunteers to help A Rocha projects in other countries. A Dutch work party visited Eastern Bohemia in 2006 to help renovate the Czech centre – National Director Pavel Svetlik is giving them instructions.

Richard Storey and Brian Cousins identifying aquatic invertebrates from the Aammiq Wetland; after working in Lebanon for two years, Richard went home to New Zealand and inspired friends and colleagues to help him establish A Rocha Aotearoa New Zealand in 2007.

The launch conference of A Rocha Peru at the Museum of Natural History at the University of San Marcos, Lima. National Director, Oscar Gonzalez, is 4th from the right.

Cruzinha, in the Algarve, Portugal, was A Rocha's first field study centre, established in 1986 by Peter and Miranda Harris and early assistant wardens.

The Alvor estuary from the air, showing Quinta da Rocha where Cruzinha, the A Rocha Portugal field study centre, is situated amongst fields and orchards.

Dr Graham McAll, a Sheffield GP, with the first electric G-wizz car to be used in the city.

The author and the Rev Dr John Stott birding on the Danube Delta, Romania, in December 2002. In the early years, when much of the church was sceptical about Christian environmental mission, John's enthusiasm for A Rocha and his public endorsement was a huge help. Discussions about a potential A Rocha project in Romania began then and still continue.

The A Rocha team in France are studying the breeding biology and hunting habits of the European Roller and taking action to protect it in the Vallée des Baux.

A Rocha Portugal began to study the European Storm-petrel in 1990, netting and ringing the birds each year as they move northwards past the coast in May and June. Now working in partnership with Dr Rob Thomas of Cardiff University, in 2007 the team ringed their 4,000th 'stormie'.

The Golden-rumped Elephant-shrew is a globally threatened mammal (the size of a small domestic cat) which occurs in the Arabuko-Sokoke Forest. It is one of many rare species on the Kenyan coast which A Rocha is working to protect.

Monarchs make amazing migrations across North America. A Rocha USA monitored their food plants in Washington DC with a team of volunteers who gained hands-on field experience.

African Pygmy Kingfisher

Daryl Bosu, Miranda Harris and Melissa Ong with other leaders at the A Rocha Kenya field study centre in Watamu, April 2007.

Rapid urbanisation is straining the relationship between people and their environment even further. For the first time in human history, over half the world's population now live in cities, compared to 30 per cent in 1950, and it is the cities of the poorer countries that are absorbing almost all the world's population growth.[7] Sustaining the resources needed for such concentrations of people is a dramatic challenge.

The form that city life is taking in the wealthy world poses a different set of relational and environmental challenges. The economic demands made on those in work have led to a social architecture that makes personal relationships stressful to sustain. Even in Canada, a country renowned for its quality of life, the average commute for 15 million Canadians is now over an hour. Even when they reach home, latest figures tell us that North Americans watch twenty-eight hours of television a week.

By contrast, Christian believing calls us to make profound local connections that will lead us to a more fruitful understanding of the places we live, whether urban or rural, or anywhere in between. During the years we lived in Portugal we became convinced that it was local belonging and involvement that led to the best ideas for the conservation of the area and the benefit of the community. So as A Rocha began to take root in other parts of the world, we determined that each person who became involved internationally should be based in a local community for his or her work; we resisted the temptation to establish a central headquarters that would be divorced from the realities of the field teams. We made this our own commitment as we settled in France and it set the pattern for the growth of the international team.

In truth, all of us have lived these commitments with some degree of tension. In our own case, the amount of travel grew much more rapidly than we had anticipated, so we have struggled with a sense of persistent unease about our choices. But we have never doubted the wisdom of taking up a locally grounded life. Here, as in so many other ways, the life of Jesus has been the conscious model for our work. He was rooted in the material and created realities of his time, yet even the most mundane and intractable of them were redeemed by the way he lived. Even as he travelled it seems he managed to be deeply local, and he was able to be completely relational even as he distanced himself from the directions that many of those around him were taking.

Throughout history, Christians have been agents of profound social transformation. Now, we could become agents of a similar environmental renewal. In the eighteenth century, the Christian conscience was awakened to the scandal of slavery; a similar awakening seems to be taking place as we come to terms with the current distress of creation and take better note of its glory. We can begin to believe that creation concerns might finally make it into the mainstream of how we live out our faith.

Christian thinking for over 150 years has struggled to find a coherent way to place our social engagement within a framework of eternal priorities. So if our new call to care for creation is not to end in a kind of dry eco-pharisaism or in another ephemeral episode in the ongoing drama of popular Christian culture, we need to understand how the log-jam originally arose. I believe it came about as we adapted the gospel to our human needs and that it will be eased as we learn to frame our lives and what we owe to creation, within a prior call to serve our Creator. To re-apply Paul's famous discourse about love in his first letter to the Corinthians, 'even if we preach about climate change, or make sure we use public transport and re-cycle our paper, it will be worth nothing if we do it for our own benefit'. It will be even worse if 'creation care' is taken on as good tactics, a shrewd move in a church effort to be relevant.

Rather, Paul's preaching and the message of the Gospels call us to respond to the Creator. The new community of God's people which forms out of love for Christ has its life within creation and the meaning of its message is manifest in all of the relationships that a created life implies. This is Christian proclamation as understood in Scripture; it can never be a matter of words alone, but neither can it be empty of explanations. The Gospels answer the questions, 'Who is Jesus and why did he live, die and rise again?' and they leave us with the question, 'If he is the Lord – of creation, of all life, of human society, of who we are – then how do we literally come to life as we recognise him as Lord?'

The very material nature of our coming to life causes Paul to revert to the image of the body when he explains how he understands the new community, telling us that we are 'the body of Christ'.[8] He understands that worship has first call on our lives, and that worship then gives identity, meaning and direction to everything else we undertake. A community that is directed towards knowing 'The God who made the world and everything in it'[9] is a far cry from an organisation that is set up to meet an artificial hierarchy of human needs.

That false hierarchy will inevitably lead to another which is as frequently evident in the most democratic of

Protestant or evangelical circles as it is in the most formal of Catholic and historic churches. If we take human needs as prior in a world where we imagine the 'spiritual' to be immaterial, then it follows that we will rank the importance of different kinds of work by dangerously false criteria. The stage will be set for an inevitable downgrading of the true significance of much human activity that glorifies God and serves his purposes. The resulting logic can only lead us to abandon the times and places in which we live, with all their uncomfortable, distressing and intractably material realities, in favour of an ill-defined but idealised future. Major sections of the New Testament are given over to arguing why it is a catastrophic wrong turning for Christian believers.

Paul's understanding of creation leads him to argue that people are therefore in an inevitable relationship to each other. 'From one man he made every nation... we are God's offspring'[10] says Paul to the motley multiracial, multi-religious crowd listening to him. There is no hint of sub-Christian 'us and them' thinking in here but rather the recognition of a true community of the created which encompasses us all.

We are in relationship with each other, regardless of race or religion or place, not because our lifestyles all impact on each other – which they do – but primarily because we share the same Creator. In recent years, it has become more evident that we share the same creation. Chinese industrial emissions affect the respiratory health of Canadians, and climate change now means that no square metre of the globe is exempt from the consequences of our way of life. But we also need to understand that the roots of global relationships are found beyond the creation in our Creator himself. The Old Testament prophets were clear that social breakdown and our neglect of the creation ultimately derive from the denial of our Creator. 'There is no faithfulness, no love, no acknowledgment of God in the land. ... Because of this the land mourns, and all who live in it waste away, the beasts of the field and the birds of the air and the fish of the sea are dying', said the ancient ecologist, Hosea.[11]

Furthermore, says Paul, where and when we live is significant. The text in Acts 17 gives us an emphasis here – although people are to 'inhabit the whole earth', God determines the exact times and places where they should live. The whole point of the conditions of time and place that frame our lives is that they cause us to reach out for God and find him. Each of our different places where we live unite us in a common search for God's purposes within them.

Paul's message is that wherever we are and whoever we are, we owe our existence to a loving God, and we will discover the meaning of our lives as we find relationship with him. Life itself, as a created gift lived in particular times and places, is going to speak to us of the Creator, if we can hear it.

Arnaud Monnoyeur wrote to us shortly before he died to explain his own conviction that the very circumstances of his life had been God's message to him. He came from a privileged family and yet, over the years, he knew several moments when in different ways he clearly heard a call to give over his life to relationship with Christ but was distracted or simply turned away. As he was a wealthy person, these calls were quite exotic: the death of a close friend swimming beside him in a pool in Venezuela, a potentially fatal fall from a building in the Philippines, the terrifying minutes on an aircraft that dropped thousands of feet over Mexico before recovering power at the last moment. He has written an account of it all in a long manuscript that makes incredibly moving reading. Here is one brief section.

> As for each one of us, although for none of us is life the same, my accidents on the journey were many. Serious car accidents – painful jungle evacuations – appalling accusations – near paralysis and death on another occasion – but God is first of all love, and I know he was always there, and yes, one of his guardian angels was surely watching over me! I wouldn't be writing this otherwise... Each time he called, but I fled ahead of him and it seemed at the age of 38 that I had it all. Even then I wanted more: my egoistic desires were for power and money – I had them both already without knowing how to enjoy or make the most of them. But once I was alone, then as I faced the prospect of dying, of course my conversion was never going to wait long. 'That's easy', they said, 'he has taken refuge in religion'. But no, it was God's intention all along through everything that happened to me, and I knew finally that what I had found was worth a hundred times more, even though now it came with the prospect of losing everything, just like Abraham on the mountain.

He was quite clear, once he began to listen to the Lord, of how the times and places of his life had been ordained so he could reach out for God and find him. He understood the plot.

Here we might consider a practical suggestion or two that can help us embrace our contexts, to challenge the disconnects and distractions that cause Christians to lose their hold on their times and places. We may want to ask ourselves if we have at least one true involvement with the material world. Do we plant anything, make anything, build anything, paint anything? What place do we have in our local community, and what are the rhythms of our life there? And then, finally, we may want to ask ourselves if we have any ongoing involvement with a problem that is intractable. Are we working with anything that we know can't be fixed but can only be lived by faith?

To embark on an examination like this may be an unfamiliar discipline, but relational audits of this kind were commonly undertaken by previous holders of the faith in a variety of different traditions. The eighteenth-century preacher George Whitefield used a daily checklist for his own well-being, and we can see that a natural understanding of his relationship to creation entered closely into the calibration of his relationship with God.

'Have I' he asked, 'after and before every deliberate conversation or action, considered how it might tend to God's glory? Have I, after any pleasure, immediately given thanks? Been recollected in eating and drinking? Thankful? Temperate in sleep?'[12] Many of us have lost the spiritual significance of such material considerations.

But Paul's emphasis in Athens on the significance of time and place should make us instantly sceptical if we hear Christians arguing that we have to make pragmatic choices between 'saving souls' and feeding the hungry – or between dealing with poverty and looking after 'the environment'. For the Christian, our believing is understood as a worshipful response to the living God who 'made the world and everything in it... the Lord of heaven and earth... [who] gives all men life and breath and everything else.'[13] We should be suspicious of artificial distinctions between 'material' and 'spiritual' needs, if for no other reason than that Paul finishes his sermon with the proclamation of Jesus' resurrection from the dead. He roots the resurrection firmly in Christ's humanity to emphasise the point. God 'commands all people everywhere to repent. For he has set a day when he will judge the world with justice by the man he has appointed. He has given proof of this to all men by raising him from the dead.' This resurrection of the body was the first manifestation of the eternally material. We affirm it frequently, but it is easy to miss its paradigmatic force for our understanding of the whole material world. In this world, God's people, the body of Christ, are seen as the first fruit of the new creation, a kind of priesthood for creation.

Of all the projects that grew out of these convictions, none seemed to make the connections between people and their given place, between people of many different faiths and cultures and a common Creator, more vividly than the work that Dave and Anne Bookless were beginning in the multicultural London borough of Southall. While we had known from earliest days that questions of belief, community and environment were closely bound together, until this vivid, urban expression of the vision began to take shape we had no idea of the real extent of those bindings.

Chapter Nine:

Common Ground in Southall

Only our religious institutions, among the mainstream organisations of Western, Asian, and indigenous societies, can say with any real conviction, and with any chance of an audience, that there is some point to life beyond accumulation.[1]

Bill McKibben

Miranda and I first met Dave and Anne Bookless when they were at the lowest point of their lives. They had arrived at Cruzinha for a short break, soon after the latest in a series of devastating miscarriages for Anne and just as the paralysing effects of the myalgic encephalomyelitis (chronic fatigue syndrome) from which she was suffering were beginning to make themselves felt. At meals round the long table, she sat in a wheelchair, sometimes unable even to grip her knife and fork. The evident delight that they shared in all the wonders of bird migration went some way towards dulling the pain, but it was there for all to see.

Miranda was deeply moved by their courage and the way they placed all of the mysteries of their story in a context of faith, despite times of real darkness. She took to spending time with Anne, while Dave and I were dealing with the waves of warblers at the bird-ringing station at the front of the house.

As so often happens, Anne and Miranda's praying and keeping of company had no immediate results, but shortly after Dave and Anne's return to England they had an extraordinary experience of healing and sensed the tide of illness and despair had begun to turn. Slowly but surely Anne's strength returned and, most wonderful of all, their first daughter was born the following year. She was the first of what was to become an extraordinary quartet of girls and, in exuberant Bookless fashion, was named Hannah Cruzinha.

As they reflected on the years of darkness they wrote: 'Anne's health is still better than at any time since 1986 – at this point we hear people saying, "Isn't God good!" Yes he is – but not only due to Anne's good health. Wasn't he the same good God when we lost our baby daughter, when Anne had painful sleepless nights, when ministering in the church felt like pushing an avalanche up hill? We've experienced a little of the amazing truth that God's goodness extends to being with us in our pain, not always taking it away, but sharing it and offering to redeem it.'[2]

As Dave and Anne's interest in A Rocha deepened, Dave agreed to join the Trustees, which in turn led to many other A Rocha people becoming familiar with the lively, multi-cultural communities of Southall where he was vicar of the Anglican parish of St George's.

If you want to navigate their main street, it is best to walk. The traffic goes forward far more slowly than the lamentable London average of nine miles an hour, now back to the same speed it achieved at the end of the nineteenth century. The smells of the crowded roads are more typical of an Indian city – cardamom and incense, cooking meats and frying samosas. There have been recent influxes of Somalis and East Europeans, but the music of the streets is still solidly Asian and the clothes stores reflect the latest Bollywood fashions. It was definitely home territory for a Bookless. Dave had spent the first ten years of his life in India and, after he married Anne, it had rapidly become her adopted culture too.

As Dave and Anne heard more about the projects that were taking shape in other parts of the world, not least from all the international A Rocha visitors who began to use their Heathrow-friendly vicarage as a handy stopover, they began to nurture the dream of establishing an A Rocha community in Southall itself. It wasn't long before they brought their ideas to Trustees' meetings. Until then noone had considered the urban possibilities for A Rocha, but they made every kind of sense. As Dave and Anne pointed out, we live in creation wherever we find ourselves and not just when we are surrounded by beautiful countryside. 'Furthermore,' Dave argued, 'the ecological footprint of London is understood to be the size of Wales, nine times the area of the city itself. But many Londoners are completely unaware of the extent of the resources from the wider creation that they are drawing on to sustain their way of life.'

So A Rocha's first field project in the UK began in a place where little previous work had been done. A range of urban environmental initiatives was started in close partnership with diverse communities. The story of what Dave and Anne have called 'a wild ride', during which they saw ninety acres of polluted waste ground transformed into the

Minet country park, the establishment of a community and offices in a cooperatively owned former nursing home, and a proliferation of educational programmes, has now been wonderfully told in their own book.[3] So here I merely wish to describe one particularly significant insight that they have brought to the worldwide A Rocha movement from multicultural Southall.

Conflict between different faith groups continues to bedevil our world. Each week brings further news of troubled places where violence erupts along fault lines that seem more than ethnic, and Southall itself has not been immune from similar outbreaks in the recent past. Communication can be a problem in an area where forty-four languages are spoken by the pupils of one reasonably typical school. Dave and Anne's four girls have at times been the only white children in their classes, but that implies no homogeneity among the others. Of course, in many places, talk of religious tension is merely a convenient mask for underlying racial, economic or social conflicts, but in Southall the expression of faith is a normal part of life for nearly all the different communities and gives an essential identity to their approach to the whole of life.

As Dave and Anne and a growing number of other team members began to take their own place within those discussions, a common concern for the local environment proved to be a strategic bridge between the various constituencies in the borough. The painstaking surveys that they undertook revealed considerable agreement about the local environmental issues and no one among the thousands of people whom they consulted showed anything but appreciation for practical Christian involvement with the polluted and degraded local area and the overcrowded spaces that were now home to so many people arriving from so many countries.

So, not only did Dave and Anne's commitment to the care of creation give their work its focus, it also provided the insight that helped them to bring people together around common tasks, and to find their own relational bearings. They developed a strong sense of belonging in a community that was first of all created by God and which only later took on different faith commitments. This fundamental, human community was one that they shared with everyone else in Southall, regardless of their beliefs.

At the same time, they discovered that their own, unequivocal, Christian commitments and convictions were the best preparation for clear and effective partnerships with others of different persuasions. To the degree that they were able to be straightforward and uncomplicated about the acknowledged differences, so they were able to enter into more appreciative relationships. Although they had heard it suggested that the best way to build inter-faith relationships was to believe in the essential unity of all faiths, they found their own approach both more honest and more welcome.

Paradoxically, the popular idea that faith differences are merely relative expressions of an underlying unity is itself a religious conviction. More than that, on closer examination it proves to be a rather patronising one. It requires that 'religion' is defined in terms of its lowest common denominator, 'the expression of faith' and, therefore, that believers in any particular creed sacrifice much that is essential to them. It assumes that 'faith' has no real reference point beyond our experience, but instead is merely something that believers find important, or helpful in coping with the challenges and mystery of life. Another version of this kind of conviction is that 'religion' is primarily a cultural phenomenon, interesting because it brings some colour into otherwise drab and uniform secular contexts, but incapable of any universal truth-telling.

It is not unusual for A Rocha to be understood as 'religious' in such misleading terms and, as the discussions with many different partner organisations of different beliefs or none began to proliferate, we were frequently grateful for the experience that we were gaining through the developing work in complex multicultural environments such as Southall, Lebanon and coastal Kenya.

We gladly take part in a wide range of conservation fora but found as we prepared to take part in a recent conference that we were encountering a set of misunderstandings from its well-meaning organisers that are typical of the contemporary, secular liberalism which frequently dominates the thinking of culturally Western institutions. They assumed that everyone agrees that beliefs of various kinds only play a part in the lives of those who declare allegiance to an organised religion. However, we were proposing an event within the conference that could examine the convictions and motivations of all those who engage in the essential work of protecting biodiversity. It seemed to us important to hold a discussion about the way in which environmental decision-making relies on values, which inevitably derive from beliefs.

In our view, belief decisions affect every conservation organisation, whether they are identified or unacknowledged, visible or unformulated. In fact, their impact is often greater if they aren't articulated and no space is made for any discussion of their role. Many have noted the 'missionary' character of the conservation movement itself as it gives programmatic form to strongly held convictions about the 'value of nature', and until quite recently it has been unusual to hear much discussion of the range of beliefs that underpin the whole enterprise.

When we proposed that a forum during the conference could examine such issues, we ran up against the organisers' conviction that the event was a belief-free zone. Their counter proposal was that a separate track should be set up for specifically 'religious' organisations to discuss such questions. That, they thought, would clearly keep 'believers' happy, while those with clearer hearts and minds could get on with objective discussions elsewhere.

To compound the confusion, it was suggested that even if such an event were to be included in the conference programme, out of respect for its Asian venue it should not be led by a Christian organisation. In blithe disregard for both demographics and the global character of A Rocha as a movement, we were asked to understand that South-East Asia was not a Christian location. Even after long discussions, we never really understood why it was more acceptable within the secular belief habitat of the organising committee to think that Asia was actually Hindu, Muslim, Zoroastrian or Buddhist, or in fact anything but Christian. Neither were we able to shift their own kind of faith, or to challenge its accompanying belief-language which used terms like the 'faith community' to divide up the landscape along lines more comfortable to the secular view.

Just as the discussions threatened to descend into philosophical farce, the problem was overcome faute de mieux by operational realities. It transpired that A Rocha was the only organisation with the capacity or readiness to work with the other potential organisers and so finally we were asked to coordinate the event on everyone's behalf.

The process confirmed something that we had learned to our chagrin during many conversations over the years at Cruzinha, namely that Christians are often perceived as being unable to work with others, even on issues of common concern. Even worse, many people believe Christian conversion is usually promoted by dishonest or manipulative methods. At the very least we need to ask ourselves why. As Dave and Anne showed, it isn't necessary to compromise your convictions about the truth of the Christian message or your belief in the importance of personal conversion in order to have trusting and wholehearted friendships with all-comers. It is ironic that secular liberalism itself displays a number of internal contradictions that frequently allow for less 'tolerance' than any of the beliefs it hopes to supplant. Even so, if we are so generally perceived as intolerant of others, Christians need to examine more carefully the ways we communicate our faith. We are suspected of having a hidden or exclusive agenda, while what we actually believe is that Christ is Lord of all the earth, which is very different.

A history of the church from its earliest days demonstrates that Christian believing is never likely to be particularly popular in wider society, and we should expect little applause from the fashionable or powerful. But underhand or aggressive evangelistic techniques are a blemish on the Christian record and they abuse the integrity of our God-given relationships. The undertow of suspicion that marked our exchanges with the organisers of the conservation conference has been present in many such conversations that we have been part of since leaving

Cruzinha. Each one has helped us to listen more wisely and to articulate our own beliefs better so we can put them on common ground in a more authentic way. But to return to 1996, as our travels resumed and we encountered new questions about A Rocha's approach in a succession of different contexts, we realised we needed to understand better how Christian belief could lead to a truly distinctive way of working in conservation.

As we took the first steps to equip ourselves to give adequate answers, we had no idea how important that clarity would become for us all. One of our current team members who confronts these questions regularly is Janice Weatherley. She works in the Brussels offices of IUCN, the World Conservation Union, and she often faces penetrating enquiries about how A Rocha's Christian identity affects our field programmes. The rest of the international team have always tried to support her as she makes the case, so we decided last year that we should reassure her friends in the office that she didn't work for a weird organisation by convening one of our regular team meetings there. They are always cheerful and robust events, so we reasoned it could only help the cause.

The good intentions all began to unravel when my back went into spasm as I lifted my case onto the train at London Waterloo. The herniated history is long and boring but suffice it to say, as many other back sufferers will understand, that at such times meetings are a trial and neither standing nor sitting is possible for long. The IUCN staff had allocated their main conference room to us and so, through its elegant glass doors, Janice's bemused colleagues could clearly see twelve A Rocha people engaged in animated discussions, while another reclined in state on one side of the conference table. We left Janice with some ground to make up in the days that followed. Now I think of it I must remember to tell her what our Finnish colleague Lennart said after he read what I have written about him in later pages: 'We have a saying in Finnish: "maine kasvaa, mutta kunnia menee", which translated means: "your reputation grows although your honour is gone."'

Janice's experience of probing questions, echoed by many other A Rocha staff, has continued to show us how important a good grasp on theology is, even for conservationists. As we gave the challenge more time ourselves, we were surprised to discover in each new experience of partnering with other conservation groups that nearly everyone has a go at theology one way or another, regardless of what they do or don't believe.

Chapter Ten:

Why Theology Matters to Tree Frogs

For this will affect every thing that is sustained
    by the Spirit
Even every thing in nature.[1]

Christopher Smart

I have a collection of theological utterances from secular or semi-believing journalists, biologists, and social commentators, all culled from this last year's papers and magazines. All are preceded by deprecating comments such as 'I am not a theologian' and are then followed by the word 'but'. It appears that theology has a bad name. It also seems to be true that even the most avowed atheists are tempted to take up its language from time to time, as is only natural in a world that constantly poses us with fundamental questions. So perhaps our choice is between using a theology that is conscious and reasonably well informed or one that comes to hand in more random fashion.

The pull to theologise while studiously pretending not to do so is not confined to decidedly secular circles but is equally evident among Christians of an activist turn of mind. The evangelical tendency is to treat theology like a wine cellar in the house of a teetotaller. We know that down there somewhere lies the product of skill and artistry, and we recognise that others may well know how to distinguish the vintages, but we wouldn't wish to go down to fetch a bottle for ourselves.

Such abstinence brings a set of advantages and disadvantages. The clear advantage is that the beliefs of activists are rapidly translated into practice and so can become quite visible through their consequences. Those who stick to water keep a clearer head and, if you never taste an argument that has gone through a complex fermentation, you can work for a while with fewer complications and greater certainties. But the disadvantage of theological abstinence is that if we take no account of how our work derives from the very nature of the God who calls us into it in the first place, then it will not be long before we are pursuing aims that are incoherent and adopting means to achieve them that are incompatible with what we believe.

The way that secular business methods and marketing techniques have found their way into normal Christian practice in the Western world provides frequent and unfortunate examples of such unreflective action. The original business paradigm that underlies the methodology takes its bearings from narrowly defined economic criteria which allow little space for a wider set of Christian considerations of the world. So even as a way of conducting business, it cannot serve truly Christian purposes without major redefinition and redemption. Yet as we go about our business or church affairs we are often in too much of a hurry, or perhaps too impressed by the values of our times, to make the effort that such a transformation would require.

Furthermore, our loosened hold on creation can make us dismissive of the material forms that our work and worship necessarily take. As we focus on the content of what we are doing, we can easily forget that its material embodiment is truly important also. It speaks eloquently of our commitments, whether it is found in our architecture, our publicity, or within any of the forms through which our lives engage with the material world.

So, Christian work in conservation needs theological clarity for its own integrity as well as to answer the questions that it begs of Christians and others alike.

Christians will begin to find their answers in worship. A worshipping community recognises very different priorities in a world which, however well intentioned, has more typically seen money and power as the exclusive keys to success in any difficult enterprise. Conservationists of all persuasions have embarked on a quest for environmental sustainability, but in the face of an acutely difficult task we all need to consider what could motivate us to achieve it.

While sustainability is an increasingly useful measure of how we should live on earth, even its most committed advocates have often recognised that as a motivation for change in human society, it seems to be lacking in power. Maurice Strong, who was Secretary General of the UN Earth Summit in Rio in 1993, said shortly afterwards that

In the final analysis, our economic and social behaviour is rooted in our deepest moral and spiritual motivations. We cannot expect to make the fundamental changes needed in our economic life unless they are based on the highest and best of our moral, spiritual and ethical traditions, a reverence for life, a respect for each other, and a commitment to responsible stewardship of the Earth. The transition to a sustainable society must be undergirded by a moral, ethical and spiritual revolution which places these values at the centre of our individual and societal lives.[2]

Ten years later, Michael Shellenberger and Ted Nordhaus were reflecting on the continuing difficulty of bringing about change in *The Death of Environmentalism* and they concluded: 'What the environmental movement needs more than anything else right now is to take a collective step back to re-think everything. We will never be able to turn things around as long as we understand our failures as essentially tactical and make proposals that are essentially technical.'[3]

In the face of the real consensus that we are confronted with dramatic environmental challenges,[4] reactions in wider Western society range from indifference, to denial, to a nihilistic refusal to change because no real transformation seems possible.

Christian thinking may have an important contribution to make at this point, but for our convictions to have any credibility or force we need to live them out, and we have hardly begun.

During our years in and around Vila Verde, it was the tangled fabric of daily life that helped us see what sustainability might begin to mean. It was the seasons of suffering and celebration that we lived with local friends which led us to call much of our own past and theirs into question, and so to see the significance of the village's history. However clearly we knew that Vila Verde would take its identity from 500 years of Moorish occupation, from the estuary that provided food and work and from the current complex relationship to the Roman Catholic Church, it was only by living there that we could begin to understand the community. In practice that meant making meals, carrying out fieldwork, sitting in meetings and getting caught up in serendipitous events that ranged from rescuing stranded vehicles in the serra to fetching elderly relatives from other villages – nothing special at all. But it was the rough texture of that life which could give visible form to the idea of what a sustainable community might look like, and which began to take us a step or two beyond theory.

So we have come to believe that the challenge to Christians is to live our own idea of sustainability, one that is fired by worship, and to see what form it can take. We might then venture some explanations.

Whatever form it takes, Christian thinking about sustainability starts from understanding it as an effect not a cause. If we believe that people can find a transforming relationship with God himself, it is that relationship which will then bring us into the wisdom and the rhythm of the personal God who created the world to be a sustainable environment. We live out all the different relationships possible to us in creation in relationship to the Creator. In biblical language, the creation was made for Christ, by Christ, and we live it in Christ.[5] As we do so, we will find sustainability must follow.

We are in possession of a great, but disregarded, treasure, the inheritance of a faith which takes hold of a loving Creator, the author of everything around us. The flattened and impoverished version which reaches us filtered through the dominant humanism of Western culture is, by contrast, not only lacking authenticity but inadequate for the current challenges of a suffering creation.

I believe that the attempt to use the idea of 'ecosystem services' to pursuade people of 'the value of nature' reflects some of the contradictions that will inevitably arise from a plainly humanist set of convictions. It expresses the pragmatism of a conservation movement that is unwilling to challenge the idea that life on earth is all about us. Lest we are tempted to feel superior, we should note that it has its exact mirror image in the appeals of preachers in many parts of the world who promise material prosperity to those who turn to Christ.

Rather, true worship of the living God is the wellspring for sustainable life. Christians care for creation, not because it is now deeply fashionable, nor because they want their grandchildren to be able to see woodpeckers in the park, or to watch deer in the countryside. For Christians it is simply a matter of a right response to God whom we have come to know as our Father and Creator, who has entrusted his earthly creation to our care. Win or lose, good weather or bad, caring for creation is an act of gratitude and can be offered up intentionally as an ongoing and vivid dialogue with the Lord of life.

This kind of environmentalism could be a gift to beleaguered conservationists in both wealthy and poor countries as they grapple with the challenge of transforming human societies. The incontrovertible evidence of systematic environmental decline seems to be affecting privileged lifestyles very little and, for the committed conservationist, this is a matter of some bewilderment. Marina Silva, Brazil's remarkable Minister of the Environment, has put it succinctly: 'We are technically super-advanced and ethically pre-historic.'[6] She went on to explain where she finds her own hope of transformation, even under the pressure of working to halt the destruction of the rain forest. 'Nothing really happens without prayer.'

Marina Silva is the daughter of an illiterate rubber tapper and still suffers the acute consequences of mercury pollution during her childhood in Amazonia. She knows better than most how wealthy and powerful decision-makers are usually well sheltered from the personal consequences of environmental degradation. But she has explained how even they are beginning to see the stress on natural resources reflected on the cost side of business equations, and she believes that the argument for change is now gaining greater leverage. Nevertheless, she has also seen on many occasions how the priority of environmental sustainability remains a hard argument to make within the protected world of the privileged.

There is a further hope that the Christian community around the world can give to the conservation movement. In the areas of the planet where biodiversity is now highly concentrated – around 2 per cent of the earth's surface holds around 70 per cent of the world's most threatened biodiversity[7] – believing communities predominate. It is remarkable how often they are Christian, but even if not, their decisions are made within an openly believing framework that can radically change lifestyles. It is therefore not surprising to read philosophers such as Max Oelschlager writing, 'My conjecture is this, there are no solutions for the systemic causes of ecocrisis, at least in democratic societies, apart from religious narrative.'[8]

Christians and others for whom belief is foundational and for whom the meaning of life is greater than a quest for personal fulfilment have shown time and again that they will change their ways if they are persuaded that this is God's calling to them.

So it is crucially important that Christians and others

understand the true significance of human choices for the well-being of wider creation. That recognition led Achim Steiner, now Director of the United Nations Environment Programme, to tell us that, in his view, 90 per cent of conservation work is with people, and so to ask, 'What, then, changes people?'

A Christian analysis of environmental destruction sees its prime cause in our broken relationship with God; we are then led into a futile quest for human fulfilment at the expense of the earth. That quest is driving the current degradation of life support for many millions of people with whom we share the planet and it is responsible for the rapid and catastrophic loss of the non-human creation. Our God-alienated state lies at the root of our problems, and our systematic self-centredness can only be met by what Jesus described as losing our lives and being born again. Good moral resolutions, solid data, wise and practical programmes, all can take us some distance of the way. But systemic effects come from systemic causes and only radical solutions will make a difference.

Probably the greatest change in environmental thinking that I have seen during the quarter century that we have been working for A Rocha has been this convergence of analysis, the agreement from both secular and Christian starting points that only a radical change of heart will do. It gives a remarkably hopeful basis for renewed understanding and partnership, so the need for clarity about what constitutes true Christian theology has never been greater for all concerned.

By the time we left Portugal, we were becoming aware that in the United States theology was playing an increasingly articulate role on both sides of arguments over the formulation of environmental policy. A number of American friends had shown an interest in our Portuguese experience, and we had seen some of the good books beginning to appear on the issue by US authors such as Wes Granberg-Michelson, Cal de Witt, Loren and Mary Ruth Wilkinson, Fred van Dyke and Dave Mahan.[9] We had also read articles by American Christians that seemed to come from another theological planet. For better or worse, American thinking was abroad in the world, and we wanted to understand what was happening on the other side of the very wide Atlantic gap.

So, in 1995, I took up the first of a series of invitations to share A Rocha's thinking with a US audience, little expecting the reactions it would provoke.

Chapter Eleven:

New Worlds

God bless the USA so large,
So friendly...[1]

W.H. Auden

In my defence, there were good reasons, if no excuses, for the rather blurred nature of A Rocha's first presentation in the United States.

We had, as usual, very little money, and in the mid nineties we understood our treasurer's admonitions about conserving the shoestring travel budget better than our need to reduce carbon emissions. As the autumn of 1995 began, Miranda and I were at Los Cocos in Argentina, but the only way we could afford the trip to the first meeting of the USA Christian Environmental Council in Colorado Springs was for me to go on alone once we had gone back to London to pick up another cheap ticket.

After three days and nights spent in a variety of buses, planes and airports, I was progressively less sure of night and day and had long ago lost any hold on logic. But, even allowing for the grievous effects of jet lag, the sharp outlines of a completely new set of responses to A Rocha's message made an immediate impression. In the following decade, I never lost my surprise that American thinking on the environment is so very distinctive.

The people I met were even more impressive than the discussions themselves. Once again, it was new friendships that really carried the A Rocha story forward.

Long before this, one hot summer afternoon at Cruzinha, we had entertained a group of Canadian young people from a tall ship moored in the bay at Ferragudo. As we showed them round, several of the students told us about the work of Au Sable, a Christian environmental institute that ran field courses in Michigan. Apparently, their charismatic director, Professor Cal de Witt, had persuaded the board of a conventional, family summer camp to invest the unexpected windfall that they had received from oil reserves under their property in encouraging environmental stewardship among a new student generation from Christian colleges. Au Sable had begun its programme of studies and teaching in 1979, and now the impact of their work was being felt in the USA and beyond through a series of good books and through their graduates who were beginning to get involved in work overseas.

When I met Cal in Colorado, he overlooked with typical generosity the evident incoherence of my explanations about A Rocha and immediately extended an invitation for our entire family to spend the following summer with his students and faculty. We were beginning to get quite used to living out of a suitcase by then and three months based by a lake hardly seemed like a hardship posting. So we gratefully accepted, knowing that we had a lot to learn about this new world of American Christian thinking.

It would be important for two reasons. Firstly, it seemed that whenever people in the environmental world went looking for the most unfortunate examples of wild-eyed Christian statements about the future of the planet, they found them in America. Some of the more vociferous apparently welcomed environmental destruction as a way of hastening the second coming and we felt we should try to understand how fellow Christians could possibly arrive at such embarrassing conclusions.

Secondly, and more seriously, we had seen in our travels how contemporary American spirituality and thinking had become a global export of enormous proportions, for better and worse. Not only in Kenya but also in Malawi and Argentina, we had encountered USA-based mission groups whose focus seemed to be exclusively on a future heaven. They were pessimistic about any hope of redemption for human society and so taught that the material conditions of life were unimportant. Christians were encouraged to be indifferent towards their material environment and we could see as we travelled that this approach was beginning to shape the attitudes of national churches and Christian organisations all over the world.

In countries with highly fragile ecosystems such as Kenya or Malawi, the results were catastrophic both for wildlife and for human well-being. While a biblical faith can be a powerful agent for the conservation and renewal of a degraded environment, a sub-biblical one is dangerous. We had seen in the rapid deforestation, soil depletion and polluted water sources of several places where Christians were in the majority that it could even be a significant driver of unsustainable living conditions for both believers and others alike.

So the global reach of the problem was not limited to the theological irresponsibility that guided the actions of a few powerful Christian individuals in the USA, even if they then influenced the policy and practice of government and multi-national corporations. It was played out in the poor environmental choices of millions of Christians worldwide who were taught no connection between their belief in a loving Creator God and their aspirations to the kind of wealth which can only be achieved by over-exploiting creation.

It would have been worth going to Colorado simply to encounter the energy and vision of Cal de Witt, which gave an entirely different impression of American leadership and wisdom. However, another friendship that began during the conference was to prove even more significant for A Rocha.

Ginny Vroblesky made the trek to Colorado Springs with the same trepidation. She came from a theologically and culturally conservative milieu in Annapolis, Maryland which, by then, had given her some uncomfortable moments during her graduate work in environmental policy. The result of all her heart-searching was a fine set of studies on the biblical teaching.[2] Many of her friends apparently felt she risked drifting into neo-paganism, but she quietly continued to follow her new convictions.

As we sat on the edge of the forest that surrounded the conference centre, she told me her story, graciously accepting my caveat that the succession of woodland birds which were all new species to my wondering eyes would inevitably be a frequent distraction as we talked. I subsequently discovered that perseverance and gentleness with the frailties of others are two of her great qualities and they would prove to be crucial gifts that she brought to leading the emerging A Rocha movement in the USA.

It was apparent that the scepticism of Ginny's church in

Annapolis had caused her some grief. So when she asked if we could come the following summer to help her organise a day conference for her friends there, we were willingly recruited.

I don't know whether we or Ginny were more surprised by the extreme range of responses that the event produced. We discovered that among church members were an expert on coral reef conservation and a family who, over three generations, had created gardens for butterflies and other wildlife in the most unpromising of suburban environments. We also had some vivid exchanges with several other church members who were less than convinced – one of the more vehement began his objections to our talk on the Sunday by announcing, 'The Reformation happened to stop people like you!'

Either way, it gave us a fine opportunity to encounter at first-hand the range of difficulties that deter many American Christians from engaging with environmental challenges.

During that first visit we identified four issues which have subsequently caused persistent problems for A Rocha in the USA. As each issue has considerable international influence, not least through its effect on the global response to climate change, I want to risk a brief examination of each one. My commentary is offered, I hope, in the most fraternal, friendly and loyal way possible and it is pure coincidence that I am writing these pages on the fourth of July.

Firstly, I have not met anyone in the US who does not believe that environmental questions are now highly politicised. Environmental preoccupations migrated in the 1960s from their starting point on the political right to their eventual adoption on the centre left, from Republicans to Democrats. Broadly speaking, until 2006 at least, that was where they found their place in the political spectrum. It seems a reverse migration is now well under way but the real problem is that an environmental discussion seems to Christians to be inevitably political and party political at that. It is even more problematic that environmental concerns are closely linked to other 'hot-button' issues, particularly those of abortion and 'family values'.

It has been pointed out to me that the causes of this political association are not as random as they seem. I was about to say that the platform can be crudely expressed as 'pro-life, anti-environment' when I remembered that the word 'crude' should be reserved for environmental logic like that which I saw when a forester at an Oregon church proudly showed me on his bumper sticker about Spotted Owls, 'If it's hootin', I'm shootin'.' So let's keep the word for when it's deserved. But what holds arguments about abortion and environment within one framework is a generalised suspicion of science itself. Many conservative Christians believe that scientific studies supporting the theory of evolution have been mobilised to attack some of their most cherished convictions. They also believe that scientific prowess has not only provided the expertise and technology for abortion but has claimed a kind of moral autonomy for the procedure.

In consequence, it has been almost impossible for scientifically based discussions of issues such as climate change, species extinction, pollution or resource depletion to gain a foothold in the subculture of the Christian right. It was here that the local programmes of action that were started by Ginny and a growing group of A Rocha supporters showed their true value. They pioneered a series of very practical initiatives – identifying the trees in their neighbourhood and linking them to the community's history, restoring Monarch butterfly habitats, introducing children to their local natural history, and many others. All succeeded in taking the focus away from politics and back into the known environment with all its importance for everyone, regardless of their views. They recruited a determined band of supporters, led by a remarkably committed and statesman-like Texan, Tom Rowley and together they spent years negotiating all the tricky stages of setting up a national organisation. They went to bird fairs, mission conferences, churches and nature centres, gradually changing the perception that Christians didn't care about what was happening to God's earth.

It was as all those conversations began that they met their second challenge, this time not political but theological, although there is a closer association between the two in the USA than in many parts of the world. Technically known as dispensational theology, it is the idea that many of God's promises are only relevant to a future age and all over the country it has a strong hold on popular Christian thinking, imagination, and biblical interpretation.

Its apocalyptic scenarios were outlined despairingly in a recent issue of *Conservation Biology* by environmental professor David Orr as a 'belief in the end times that tends to make evangelical Christians careless stewards of our forests, soils, wildlife, air, water, seas and climate'. He went on to assert that 'Evangelicals' belief in the end times has the paradoxical effect of seeming to justify behaviour that brings on the end times, but of a sort without scriptural basis.'[3] It is a poor state of affairs when a secular critic is able so perceptively to call the attention of the Christian world to its own theological deficiencies. Happily, he also opened the way for a senior and international group of scientists to introduce the journal's readers to a more measured and accurate review of evangelical Christian thinking on the question in a paper entitled 'Conservation Theology for Conservation Biologists'.[4] Truth is no one's enemy.

The third marker in this whistle-stop analysis is the bad-tempered argument between creationists and evolutionists. I would hate to give it any more air time, and furthermore I am, like the vast majority of those who have so fruitlessly engaged in it, technically unqualified in the relevant academic disciplines that are needed by anyone wishing to make any meaningful contribution. So I merely observe that one consequence has been to drive many Christians away from a career in the environmental sciences, much as they have been deterred from continuing in obstetrics and gynaecology by the ferocity of the arguments over abortion.

There are more positive reasons why biologically-minded Christians have preferred to enter medicine rather than conservation or the environmental sciences, such as the encouragement their pastors give them based on the concern for people's well-being, which has always been a part of the Christian tradition. It is only rarely that pastors or other Christian leaders express any such enthusiasm for the well-being of the wider creation, and their extensive influence in the USA provides little impetus for people to see work for conservation, or environmental careers, as an equally vital expression of Christian vocation and mission.

Here again the way that A Rocha USA was able to mobilise volunteers to go and help overseas projects enabled churches to see exactly how such work was an important and strategic calling. The people who began to get involved ranged from the experts in geographical information systems who gave technical assistance in Portugal, taxonomists who went to help the team in Kenya and carpenters who helped renovate the centres in the Czech Republic and France. From the beginning, the USA vision brought much-needed resources to many places.

The final issue that A Rocha in the USA frequently encountered was the one that was most painful of all, both for them and for their international friends. As they began to take their message out into different churches around the country, they were constantly confronted by a widespread confusion between the American way of life and the core of the Christian faith. They introduced the leader of a major national evangelical movement to his equivalent in the conservation world, only to hear him affirm 'free-market economics' as one of the three essential, evangelical beliefs of his organisation. Commitments of that kind have left the church throughout the USA particularly vulnerable to attempts to baptise a particular national culture. The especially privileged lifestyle that so many enjoy, but from which millions of others in the country are excluded, is sometimes seen as an expression of the kingdom of God. It then becomes particularly difficult to challenge the hold that materialism and individualism – both so fundamental to common American thinking about wealth – has on the church. Neither has any place within a biblical vision of the stewardship of creation, they are incompatible with a serious attempt to find global sustainability, and they wreak even greater havoc when exported to the church around the world.

Bill McKibben is one of the most perceptive environmental commentators in the USA today. He has pointed out the irony of this situation in writing, 'At its truest, religion represents the one force in our society that can postulate some goal other than accumulation. In an idolatrous culture, religion can play a subversive role. Churches, mosques, and synagogues almost alone among our official institutions can say, It's not the economy, stupid. It's your life. It's learning that there's some other center to the universe.'5

Materialism and individualism in twentieth-century America have been given a clothing of theological rags much as apartheid disguised its naked error with sub-biblical theologies in twentieth-century South Africa. In truth, no other national church can point any fingers; we are all capable of swimming unthinkingly downstream in the polluted waters of our culture and times and no one can claim high ground on the banks above the current. All we can do is take full advantage of the cross-cultural and therefore counter-cultural perspectives of the worldwide body of Christ to avoid drowning or being swept away.

Quite apart from the prophetic presence and voices of innumerable local churches, there are also fine resource organisations such as the Center for Public Justice in the USA, the Kairos Institute in Argentina, or the London Institute for Contemporary Christianity in the UK to help us. Such listening to each other, and any profound engagement in each other's lives, is very hard but necessary.

Sometimes the simplest and least complicated message is the hardest of all. When Matthew and Nancy Sleeth, who now lead A Rocha USA, became Christians, they soon concluded that their lives had to change. So they sold their house and large car, and downsized: Matthew gave up his work as a medic and Nancy as a teacher so that they could campaign for creation. They make it sound simple, but the changes for them and their family have been truly profound as recounted in Matthew's wonderful book *Serve God, Save the Planet*.[6] They showed us all that we have to live our discipleship culturally but we cannot do so casually and so we need to be intentional if we are to avoid the shame of falsely representing the gospel of Christ.

Undoubtedly this is no easier or harder for Christians throughout the USA than others in the rest of the world. They are not helped by the cultural isolation of much of the domestic media which have left many across the country apparently oblivious to the acute environmental stress of the poorer world. So when a different perspective arrives for the first time, it can be hard for both listeners and speakers alike to bridge the gap in perceptions that has opened up.

It was probably somewhat quixotic for Miranda and me to get involved at all in such a major set of issues, but two reasons continued to draw us in. The first was that we wished to be faithful to the deepening relationships with a growing number of friends of A Rocha in the USA, not least those who were soon contributing their volunteer skills around the world. The second was simply that funding for many Christian initiatives in many countries comes from the generosity of USA donors. A Rocha faced a growing set of acute financial challenges in so many places that a dialogue with potential partners on their behalf became inevitable and it rapidly led to other discussions and invitations.

The fundraising part of the discussions proved highly

frustrating at times, so I entertained some harmless little strategies to make it tolerable. From the distance of our new office in France at the end of long, working afternoons when I was aware life was beginning to stir across the Atlantic, I was sometimes unable to resist the temptation to call up some of the conservative Christian foundations that can be found so easily on the internet.

'Good morning, Christian Missions Funding International. How can I help you?'

'Hello. I am calling from A Rocha, an international Christian environmental organisation.'

'Good to hear you. But we are a Christian missions funding group.'

'Yes, and actually that is why I am calling, because we are a Christian mission and we certainly need funding.'

'I'm sorry, I thought you said you were an environmental organisation?'

'Yes, I did, or if you like, you could say we are a Christian environmental mission.'

'But we only fund Christian work, not environmental work, so I believe you have the wrong number?'

After a further few minutes of mutual incomprehension and maybe at best some tentative theological exchanges or at its worst some surreptitious quote collection on my part (and maybe on theirs, who knows?), I would ring off feeling unaccountably cheered.

In the early days of planning an A Rocha centre in the States, there were some fears that once the American Christian world discovered what A Rocha was doing, there would be such an explosion of initiatives and energy that the whole movement would be engulfed by American culture and resources. The opposite proved to be the case.

Ginny slowly built a network of people, many of them environmental professionals, but like her they were battling both with incomprehension from their Christian friends and also hostility towards evangelicals among their environmental colleagues. The latter were incredulous about what they were hearing from some of the more vehement and politically aligned leaders of Christian organisations and 'policy institutes' who were not only opposed to measures that would counter climate change or species extinction, but were just as happy to go on the record with vehement attacks on fellow Christians. While I have plenty of references that document this extremely sad state of affairs, in the interests of Christian unity and peacemaking, I think it is better to keep them out of the bibliography.

It was possibly as a result of this difficult context that the people in the emerging A Rocha network, scattered across the country, spent their early years getting to know each other through small local projects and meetings, praying and grappling with the challenge of how to think clearly about what to do. This long and prayerful period laid the foundations for the explosion of interest and activity that is now going on all over the country, but it was a salutary lesson for the whole A Rocha family. We soon discovered that our initial role was to be supportive of our brothers and sisters who were battling away in a very complicated situation, and that we shouldn't expect Americans to provide the solutions for our own needs for help.

Any book will be a fossil. It is laid down breathing on the stratum of time that happens to be on the surface at the moment it is completed; this one is no exception. No other context for A Rocha is changing faster than the USA one and maybe no other change is destined to have a greater impact on environmental conditions worldwide.

Chapter Twelve:

Going Global

The ideal of the modern corporation is to be (in terms of its own advantage) anywhere and (in terms of local accountability) nowhere.[1]

Wendell Berry

I began to understand what it would mean for A Rocha to become a global organisation when I saw Markku Kostamo from Canada in lively discussion with Vijay Anand from India at the first leaders' conference in France in 1999. It was not just a question of being international, because we always were that from the very start. Nor was it just the challenge of keeping a cross-cultural identity as we grew, although it took intentional effort, as we made key decisions, to avoid defaulting into Anglo-Saxon assumptions. It was more that we needed to find a way of making global relationships work in a truly personal and not merely institutional way.

The organisation was growing rapidly by this point, and the distances at which we all worked from each other were becoming greater all the time. We were arriving at the end of a millennium but that wasn't what prompted us to think even harder about the shape of our future. Rather, it was the growing number of increasingly different national expressions of the A Rocha vision.

In Canada, Markku and his wife Leah had put their entire savings into the adventure of securing the new field study centre that they were establishing with a team of others near White Rock, just south of Vancouver. As they tried to coordinate the efforts and interests of people across a vast country, separated by thousands of miles and four time zones, they faced many questions that were similar to those we had to answer for A Rocha as a whole. At the same time, they and their team were running a robust local programme that included salmon stream restoration projects, downtown environmental education camps in the deprived east side of Vancouver and, yes, looking after the cattle. They embarked on sustainable agriculture and the numbers of people joining them grew as fast as their pumpkins, rapidly reaching twelve or more full-time staff and hosts of volunteers. So they were very busy on site and in their own neighbourhood – but had to take account of the enthusiasms of people thousands of miles away. The entrepreneurial and pioneer nature of their members soon prompted them to propose another centre, as the unstoppable energies and hospitable instincts of Henry and Elma Martens led them to hand over their home and a large protected area that they had established so that it could become the A Rocha Pembina Valley centre in Manitoba. In other words, everyone involved was welcoming the necessary tension of sustaining an intensely busy community life and a very wide range of local involvements, while being simultaneously committed to many other relationships over long distances. It all reinforced the model with which we are still working – locally incarnate leadership for a very widely dispersed organisation.

Meanwhile, even the meaning of community within A Rocha was developing fast as different expressions emerged, while the original form it had taken at Cruzinha remained an important source of inspiration for many visitors from other countries.

Ginny Vroblesky had written to us from Annapolis on her return from her own visit:

> Our real need was to learn from A Rocha in Portugal how to draw people into community working together on a project, to affirm their worth. I had remembered how a fellow student at grad school had been distressed that she had only learned from a Muslim that Christianity had been the mix out of which good science could grow. She had been taught her whole life that religion was irrelevant to a scientist. Conservation itself was not our big need in the USA. We had many organizations here already doing good conservation work. But there were not many which had the potential to touch people in the way that A Rocha did.

As the months passed, we heard from yet more people who wanted to begin projects in their own countries. While we had met, or worked with, all of the early generation of A Rocha leaders, our first contact now with many people was by email. They had found A Rocha on the internet, or met former A Rocha visitors and staff as they had dispersed around the world. In the face of increasing travel to existing teams, a growing number of new requests for help and ever more invitations to visit potential projects, the international team faced a choice. Should we limit our efforts to simply encouraging these fellow Christians to set up their own kind of work and just exchange news from time to time? Or was there a way to bring them into A Rocha, even if it meant an even greater number of new national organisations? We were already finding it hard enough to sustain programmatic efficiency as we were growing so fast; how could we keep personal relationships at the heart of what we were doing in a larger organisation?

Communicating by internet was just beginning to be a real possibility even for those in poorer countries and it seemed to offer some solutions. Email and virtually free computer phoning could keep the costs of exchanging information quite low. But it was clear that no one in A Rocha wanted to belong to a faceless corporation; neither did we believe that we should really encourage anyone to spend more time on long-distance relationships than with the people around them. Closer to my own home, I found that I needed to use the phrase 'virtual community' with great caution if Miranda was anywhere nearby, unless I was ready for instant high-voltage debate, fuelled by her reading of Neil Postman and other technology critics. His prescient title *Amusing Ourselves to Death* might have served well for some of the lengthy and heated discussions that the internet was provoking in our own far from virtual community. We concluded that even if the environmental and financial costs of travel were high, A Rocha's emerging leaders around the world needed real time with others if we were to form our global vision together. The exchange of information might be cheap and necessary but building relationships would be expensive and vital.

As we adopted different media, we began to understand that we had to be very intentional about which we used for what purpose. After a hard look at the gains and losses, we realised that if some media allow for communication in particular ways, they prohibit it in others. When we ran into disagreements or hurts with those at a distance, as is inevitable with any group of people that works together, email was the worst of ways to make progress towards understanding and usually proved positively inflammatory. We also found that if we wanted people to learn about A Rocha in a transformational way, simply mailing out materials would never be enough. Local and personal involvement didn't just make sense as the basis for our work, it was the best foundation for growth strategy. Time spent emailing or on Skype conference calls is time lost to the people and the place around you.

The emails that arrived from people like Oscar Gonzales in Peru or Moses Kofi Sam in Ghana consistently told the same story. They knew very few others in their national churches who felt that environmental concerns had anything to do with Christian belief, so they badly needed the fellowship and support of people who shared the same convictions and passions. They wanted their projects to belong within A Rocha because they felt very isolated. A distant networking exercise wouldn't meet their needs, so we could see that the only alternative was to create a kind of global family.

If sustaining our personal relationships was to be an integral part of A Rocha's approach to environmental work, it was obvious that we would need to get used to the idea of more travel. We tried to give serious thought to how we could do that in a way that honoured the commitments to people and creation that we were endeavouring to live by.

During our time at Cruzinha we only travelled every couple of years, while over the last decade it has sometimes seemed that we are leaving for somewhere every couple of weeks. But in one sense nothing of personal significance has changed. We have always known that the only life worth living is in response to God, open to being shaped by what he loves and formed in both the detail and the broad sweep of his purposes. So the change from a very local existence to more travelling than we often felt we could handle was only a change of canvas for the same palette of truths.

On the other hand, as we understood better that time and place are created gifts of God and that the material context of life is his handiwork, we had to recognise the consequences of these realities for how we lived. Constant travel has certainly made it much harder to keep faith with our friends and to hold clearly to a vision of life that is grounded in a local context. In struggling to make it work better, we have developed a number of strategies which may resonate with others who now have a lot of travel in their lives, or who have found themselves uprooted and somehow lost in translation.

Firstly, we endeavour to keep community and, whenever possible, to stay with friends or colleagues rather than in the convenient and often more comfortable two stars that are the standard accommodation for NGO staff on mission. Then, as we go, we try to remain personal with the people we find alongside us on trains, buses, planes and the inevitable waiting lines, and to be intentional in all the relationships we find there. Our life at Cruzinha had been full of the complete unpredictability of comings and goings of a busy field study centre. So we had needed to learn how to give clear signals and either to be present to people, or to be clear that we couldn't be, rather than being physically there but mentally elsewhere. We now try to live the travels the same way. Travelling makes you blurry, so I have to say that the intentions have only partly succeeded, for me at any rate. But whenever we take the extra time to make sure all our relationships remain human and are not reduced to the functional, it is a small act of resistance against the impersonalisation of life that can have startling and heart-warming consequences.

Secondly, I have needed to acknowledge my difficulty in recognising the real limits to time and to accept those limits as a gift not a frustration. There is a rich tradition of Christian thinking that agrees with Athanasius who said that 'busyness is moral sloth'. If we take all that we are given to do by faith and know that all of it matters to God, then we must surely believe that we are given the time for all that we need to do. I have realised recently that I live with a kind of fear (panic would not be too strong a word) that I will never have the time for all I want to do. Recognising that has helped me realise that it is usually what I want to get done that is out of kilter, and not the Lord's requirements of my time. So I have reluctantly added rush and procrastination, and the stress that comes from both of them, to a list of the abuses of creation.

The abuse of time matters because, eventually, it will damage our other relationships with people and with the creation. As A Rocha has entered into partnership with other organisations that have embraced a culture of over-working, it has not always been easy to keep our bearings and to match the different expectations. The tyranny of the urgent is an epidemic condition in many Western NGOs, as one might expect in organisations where gifted and highly committed people are trying to do very difficult work, frequently with very scarce resources. So, part of our survival strategy has been to begin by being realistic about the amount of time a given project will take, which is usually at least three times longer than we anticipate. After all those projects, why should there be any surprises there?

Christians should certainly be at an advantage in this; after all, our history places events such as the crossing of the Red Sea in the centre of our tradition. We, more than anyone, should know that we aren't the ones who will actually bring about the transforming moments, the times when our work takes a big step forward. Ours are not the only rhythms in play, and our pace isn't the only one that counts. If we can attend to the intentions of the Creator we will have found a better way of living and working with the grain of his creation.

So in very practical terms, we have tried to make travelling well a process of understanding God better, in how he has made the world and in how he has created both time and distance. If people who are working passionately for the care of creation deny the created limitations of time and of their energies, then it is not simply ironic; we are courting relational and personal wreckage.

As well as the length and number of journeys, the size of the rapidly developing organisation was also beginning to give us serious pause for thought. Our commitment to creation was a commitment to the form A Rocha was taking and not just to a message, so we needed to reorganise in order to cope. It put us on a steep learning curve as we agreed that the number of people getting involved could only grow at the organic pace that truly human relationships need. So Graham Wright, one of our Trustees, hastily developed a set of guidelines for new national organisations. In the process he demonstrated how intellectual capital and a reckless volunteer commitment to burning the midnight oil would always be a precious gift at A Rocha's key moments. In subsequent years, the guidelines were followed as scrupulously as anyone could have wished and were subject to constant revision. Even so, in the heady days of 2003, the international Trustees recognised four new national A Rocha organisations during one meeting, after only two hours of discussion.

A friend in another organisation once told me that inertia settled on their plans whenever their committee had to make decisions and asked me how it was that A Rocha didn't seem to be slowing down. The honest answer was that we seem to have been blessed with a set of Trustees who are adrenaline junkies but who have deeply sceptical and locked-tight financial and legal minds. The group is made up of about ten men and women from five or six different countries, and they commit to us for up to nine years. They meet twice a year for at least two days at a time so that they can engage prayerfully and trustingly with the issues. Many of the early UK-based group had international experience, so as we internationalised it was an almost seamless transition to the current multicultural committee. Once again, the strong friendships that have characterised the group have been very important, and have meant that the robust disagreements in which they seem to take a particular delight are carried out with great good humour.

In this group too there has been some grieving, as there was for the A Rocha team in France when we lost Arnaud to cancer. Miranda and I had known Alan Coverdale since our days as students in Cambridge together. We risked our close friendship when we asked him to take on the leadership of the Trustees after their first decade under Bob Pullen's chairmanship, but it seemed to more than survive all the tough choices and decisions he led us through. Alan had spent his working life in the British government's aid programme, and it was almost certainly his years in Africa that caused the malignant melanoma he developed in his early forties. His death in 2000, even more poignant after only fifteen months of marriage to Sandra, was a huge loss to us all, and his irreverent economist's commentary on our brighter ideas still seems to echo around the current discussions at times. His iconoclastic style of chairing the Trustees was taken up later by Matthias Stiefel, whose extraordinary life really deserves a book of its own.

We first met Matthias in the mid eighties when he was taking a career break from work as a political scientist in the UN and was subsistence farming in the Algarve, while bringing up his two small children. As he tells it, he was aware that through pressure of work, constant travel and the stress of many things in his life that were failing to hold together, he was losing his soul, without truly knowing what his soul was. Through meeting a Reuters journalist who went down to the south of Portugal to find out what had persuaded one of the UN's brightest and best to give it all up, he also met Christians and his searches found some of their answers in a deep relationship with Christ. He also married the journalist, Rebecca, and they eventually returned to Geneva and the working mainstream. Over the years that followed, they opened doors in many remarkable ways for A Rocha all over the world and, in addition, Matthias' unique combination of extreme Swiss attention to detail and Italian flair helped the Trustees to navigate all kinds of interesting moments with equanimity and grace.

The arrival of David and Betty Payne was another enormous encouragement as we battled to work out what kind of an organisation we would need to become in order to make the most of all the multicultural energy and creativity that was pouring into A Rocha. They had spent most of their lives in East Africa where Betty had been born and where David then worked in rural development projects. A new partnership with the missions group, Crosslinks, brought them to A Rocha at a crucial moment. David had chaired the Trustees in earlier years so already knew the organisation well. At the same time, Betty brought a timely and remarkable gift of hospitality to A Rocha just as it was needed. The number of people on the international team was growing fast and, with her talent for home-making and providing abundant meals, she made their home our own as the team spent time together in meetings. It wasn't long before many other A Rocha people from around the world were finding their way to David and Betty's door, to a warm welcome and wise counsel.

David's clear, strategic thinking and administrative gifts brought order out of all the improvising which had been our necessary idiom until his arrival in 1998. To our cost, we had already begun to see how our inability to provide clear policy for the proliferating family of projects could be as much a cause of damaged relationships as any of the more obviously ill-intentioned human behaviour of which we are all capable. We were never exempt from that either, as we are all lamentably flawed as people, but we were certainly spared many potential meltdowns by David's wise leadership as our Managing Director over the years that followed.

As David began to document our accumulating experience and turn it into proposals for good practice, he was often faced with the problem that what had worked in one country rarely seemed to transfer very readily to another. His case studies often seemed to be outnumbered by an equal list of the exceptional circumstances that were built into the history of each new project. We also became aware that as the national organisations grew, they were beginning to need other leaders with team building or management skills who could complement the early pioneers. Managers became ever increasingly important as the work began to get more extensive and complex, but funding such people was never easy.

A new organisational model continued to develop in order to support all this burgeoning activity. Thematic leadership began to emerge and Will Simonson was invited to rejoin A Rocha in 2001 to give coordination and leadership to the scientific programmes. Together with Rachel, whom he had married the year before she set up our first international office in Cambridge in 1995, he moved to Portugal to be based within the national team. Both of them brought wise cross-cultural skills that were soon needed elsewhere as well, and Will took on the liaison with the Ghanaian group when the time came to make the first site visits. Will and Rachel's 'yellow house' in Vila Verde, the gift of another A Rocha supporter, saw a stream of visitors arrive at the door and it soon provided another welcoming home for the meetings of the international team. It was deeply moving to witness Rachel's immediate care for so many of the friends that Miranda had made when we had moved to the village in 1984, and to see the way that all the family quickly found their place in local life and in the Cruzinha team.

Many people continued to arrive there from all over the world but, even so, if the seeds for the first generation of A Rocha projects had been sown by a diaspora of Cruzinha staff and visitors, the next generation were largely blown by the wind of the internet.

As we went beyond the initial contacts by email to the first visits to the emerging A Rocha groups in each country, we soon learned the limitations of internet reality and the expectations it would give us. Our first encounter with Lennart Saari, guiding spark of A Rocha Finland, was an early indication of what would follow in many places.

Chapter Thirteen:

The Turning Tide on Many Shores

There are known knowns. These are things we know that we know. There are known unknowns. That is to say, there are things that we know we don't know. But there are also unknown unknowns. There are things we don't know we don't know.[1]

Donald Rumsfeld

Well, we knew of Lennart's legendary commitment to field-work. He had just completed twenty-seven years of continuous ornithological studies on his beloved island of Aasla in the Baltic archipelago. Each year he had put in between two and three hundred full days of field surveys, in all weathers and in all seasons, on this beautiful four-mile-long rock which had been home to his family for some generations. We knew he had thought deeply about how his Christian faith shaped his work and about the marked indifference of many in the Finnish churches to environmental issues. As over 80 per cent of Finns would identify themselves as Lutherans, there was clearly enormous potential for change throughout the country if they did begin to consider the question more seriously. Even worldwide the effect would be considerable, as Finland has a higher percentage of overseas mission people, per capita, than any other country. Many of the questions that Lennart had raised in our early flurry of email exchanges seemed to be culture specific, so as I prepared to visit him for the first time I persuaded Markku Kostamo from A Rocha Canada to join me. Perhaps he could reach back into his Finnish origins to help the discussions along?

Markku and I were feeling reasonably well prepared as we arrived together in Helsinki at the beginning of the week's exploratory programme that had been sketched out for us. Even so, Lennart's opening gambit as he met us at the airport was a surprise.

'Well,' he said, 'all my friends are absolutely astonished that I have even managed to organise a few meetings. I hope you realise I am surely not the person to do anything like this.' Finnish humour is in a league of its own, and I was still catching up, but by the end of the week we knew it was one of the few times that Lennart had been in earnest.

We also soon discovered how he had survived the rigours of his fieldwork: he ate rather like the birds of prey with whom he shared his island, very occasionally, but when the chance arose, very comprehensively. As we began by travelling round the universities and churches of several different cities, we could see that he had chosen our accommodation principally by whether a buffet-style breakfast was part of the deal. As we left each one, it was clear they would be rapidly revising their arrangements after they had watched in awe as Lennart fired up his metabolism for the lean days of fieldwork ahead.

I learned to adjust my own gastronomic expectations as the trip continued. On the third morning, as we prepared to set out from his cabin for a pre-dawn sortie, fasting seemed once again to be the order of the day so I murmured something about breakfast. We Brits specialise in murmuring at such moments.

'Ah yes,' mused Lennart, 'breakfast... well, you could certainly look in the freezer. There is probably chocolate ice cream – but then, mind how you open the door, as my daughters usually set it all up to fall out on top of me... Finnish humour you know...'

Somehow it was Finnish cuisine which really dominated the various sagas of the trip – Lennart even took us to meet the philanthropically-minded owner of a national hamburger chain who he thought was his best hope for providing some start-up funding for his plans. Thankfully, he didn't own the roadside van that supplied the supper which made Lennart so ill for the last few days we were together.

Lennart's final flourish came on the closing evening of our tour as he made a detour en route to Helsinki via the impressive cathedral in Turku.

'As our time together is ending,' he said with quiet pride, 'I have organised that we meet with some women who surely know how to pray. They are a small group, but they are really quite something and they are really absolutely enthusiastic for what we are planning with A Rocha Finland.'

It seemed a great idea, but we couldn't help noticing that we were arriving along with a crowd of about 500 others who were streaming through the doors of the building. We asked Lennart what was going on.

'Yes, well after we have prayed with the ladies, you will preach for an hour or so to these others if that is OK?'

A keen look at his absent-minded smile was all it took to see that this wasn't in the category of Finnish humour but of Saari organisation.

Our first visits to other countries similarly revised any preconceived expectations we gained from the fragmented emails that preceded them. A Rocha Peru is working in the kind of spontaneous Latin culture that we came to love in Portugal, yet the week we spent in Lima with Oscar and Marlene Gonzalez and their newly formed committee was planned to the minute.

They organised a four-day conference at the Museum of Natural History in the University of San Marcos, Lima, for the formal launch of the project, bringing together ornithologists from all over the country. Oscar had also selected several potential project sites for us to visit during our week together. We might have imagined that the new Peruvian group would be planning a focus on the treasures of the Andes or the rainforest. Yet the places we were shown were small wetlands on the edge of the city, and even a tiny area of wooded habitat that Oscar had painstakingly created over the last twenty years in an open city block behind his house. As we left after an action-packed week, we had to confess to a tiny disappointment that during our time in a country with over 1700 bird species on its national list, we had seen no more than forty or so, but it seemed that A Rocha's newest members had truly understood how we should all be working. Oscar and his team had made their choices for initial projects in the hope that they could work with some of Lima's poorest people; in a city of 8 million almost entirely without green spaces, it seemed like the kind of ornithology of which Jesus would approve.

Even the political side of the programme had been effectively covered by a set of meetings with senior people in government and the churches and with the leaders of other NGOs who would need to give their approval to any future partnerships. Life in Portugal had prepared us for the importance of courtesy and protocol, so we felt quite at home going from office to office in a series of dilapidated taxis, five of us at times crowding into the back seat to make the most of the limited funds we had scraped together for the programme.

Thankfully, the whole trip was extremely energising, although it's possible we unknowingly had some additional help from Oscar's father. Now in his nineties, he is the youngest of twenty-one children, and has lived a remarkable life as a doctor in some of Peru's most deprived communities and as a botanist in some of the country's most remote areas. Each morning at breakfast, after greeting us in boisterous French, he went out into his garden to collect the berries of a plant he had brought back from the high Andes to make us a strong, hot drink. We never discovered whether it really was a new strain of coffee, as he claimed, or whether it was something slightly more stimulating but, either way, the day seemed to go very well from then onwards until energy levels mysteriously crashed in the late afternoon.

Sofia was another capital city where an A Rocha group had been forming and that was long overdue for a first visit. We had Frédéric Baudin and the long-established cultural ties between France and Bulgaria to thank for the poignant email that had arrived one day from Adelina Timova. She and other friends in her church had been tackling the pollution and abandonment of the small rivers that run through the capital. They wanted to set up nature trails for children in the parks but no one in their churches seemed interested. Could we help? Her email ended, 'We won't hide the truth from you that there is no one we could rely on, only God. He has been faithful to us till now and he is going to be because he is our father and he cares for his creation.'

Once again, another A Rocha member with years of experience in the country, Helen Parry, was able to give time to act as cultural and linguistic interpreter for the trip. We discovered as soon as we arrived that everyone who had been involved in organising the activities of the group so far was battling in some way to hold their lives together: living in tiny apartments with elderly relatives, or holding down jobs that demanded long hours for minimal return. Even so, they were not short of ambition or hope for their environmental projects, which they planned to fund through a series of business initiatives in eco-tourism. They could see a lot of possibilities for groups to visit some of the spectacular sites for wildlife and plants around the country and, soon after we returned, Barbara Mearns, our International Administrator, began to plan a tour for A Rocha members from the Netherlands and the UK which proved a great success. Subsequently, the group has struggled to make much progress and has remained small; a key member emigrated, and those who remain have found the pressures of daily life too great to allow for much voluntary effort. Currently they are running a peony conservation project with some success, but they are convinced that until they can find a way to take on full-time team members it will be very difficult to go much further and overcome the limitations imposed by doing everything on a volunteer basis.

The experience of the group in the Czech Republic seemed to show the benefits gaining full-time leadership early in the story. We first heard about them in a careful, handwritten letter from Pavel Svetlik that proved the exception to the email rule. He was clearly a paid-up member of that international fraternity of bird ringers who are entranced by the mysteries of migration – he thought it was even possible that one of the Kingfishers we had caught at Cruzinha bearing a ring from the Czech Republic had been ringed by him in the eighties. He was very well respected for both his fieldwork and the range of activities that he and his wife Radka had been running for decades with schoolchildren, taking them out into the countryside to construct nest boxes for dippers or to learn to identify birds by their songs and calls. However, it seemed that only one other leader in the country really felt this was a proper concern for a pastor: most church people felt he should be preparing people for heaven by turning their gaze away from life on earth. As the earth, in their part of the world at least, had been so degraded and polluted by the systematic exploitation of the Communist years, it was tempting to believe that redemption played no part in its future. But Pavel's studies of both the apostle Paul's letter to the Romans and Czech birds wouldn't allow him such an escapist position. Given that he had been involved in thirty years of studies revealing that Little Owl populations in the country had crashed from 10,000 pairs to just 200 pairs, his tenacious hope was even more remarkable.

Happily we already knew his one great supporter (who was inevitably also called Pavel, but this time surnamed Cerny). We had met him some years earlier when he was working on his doctorate in the UK, and even then he had been enthusiastic about A Rocha's ideas. Now he had become the President of the Czech Brethren Church and was even keener to help. When we met in Prague, he told us, 'We are already providing a chaplain for the army. Without doubt the most important issue for our country is our environment, and so Christians should be playing an active role in that, too.' So he and his council agreed to continue funding Pavel's salary as he moved from being a pastor to lead the emerging A Rocha movement throughout the country.

Together the two Pavels soon identified others to help advise the emerging group. Their first board chair (ah yes, another Pavel, but this time Stifter) was a well-known local politician of great Christian maturity and some scientific stature. His own contribution to natural history was rather less visible – a world-class collection of microscopically sized water fleas. I took it on trust that they were spectacular and just hoped that A Rocha Czech wouldn't decide that fighting for their conservation should be the focus of their efforts. Fundraising was difficult enough for beautiful and emblematic birds like the Rollers we were beginning to study in the Vallée des Baux, but passionate appeals for threatened fleas would take us into completely uncharted territory.

No such difficulties would attend the species that was the speciality of Vijay Anand from Bangalore. He was completing his PhD on Asian Elephants and was hoping to find some new ways of dealing with the acute conflicts that were developing between the animals and the villagers around the Bannerghatta National Park. He had first been introduced to A Rocha by one of our international Trustees, Simon Stuart, who had told us of Vijay's very practical Christian faith and his abilities as a researcher and manager.

We saw both talents in action as, together with a number of other gifted people (including Prem Mitra, who was pastoring a local Anglican church and who was to become the first chairman of the national committee), he organised a launching conference for A Rocha India which brought together top level scientists and Christian leaders. Among the speakers who were both was another international trustee, Sir Ghillean Prance, one of the world's leading botanists. He had spent considerable time working in India where he had many friends, although his ties weren't as strong as the ones Simon had through his adopted daughter, Jyoti.

Ghillean and Dave Bookless brought presentations to show the commitments of the wider A Rocha family that this newest movement was joining, and gave an idea of how we would want to support them in the challenges of beginning an entirely new national organisation. We were grateful for the international character of so many of the A Rocha leaders, but would puzzle over the next few years about how to make such widely separated teams work well together. Thankfully the A Rocha India group showed incredible endurance, and all of Vijay's family, not least Sunita his wife, were soon involved in the effort. It wasn't long before they had started a whole range of activities, and were mobilising more volunteers than any other A Rocha group anywhere in the world. They did it simply through commitment and imagination with virtually no initial funding.

The group in South Africa followed a similar pattern of simply beginning work and doing all they could until funds arrived. Their priorities under the guidance of Allen and Joyann Goddard, the ornithologist Mark Brown and a small group of other supporters around the country, took them into involvement with informal settlements and urban communities where poverty and conservation seemed at first to be running into headlong collision. The Msunduzi River runs through Pietermaritzburg and as well as being the venue for a world-famous canoe marathon, it is important for many wildlife habitats and species. It suffers from high levels of pollution due to the rapid urbanisation of its banks by informal settlements and huge rubbish dumps that spill vast quantities of toxic waste into the water. Allen and his team, in partnership with municipalities and other organisations, have begun a series of initiatives that range from replanting riparian woodland to community education through the churches. They believe they can create a true sign of hope in the heart of the city; slowly their message is beginning to spread and other groups are forming elsewhere to begin their own projects.

A similar set of almost overwhelming challenges were spelt out to us in an email that arrived from Moses Kofi Sam, who was working in Ghana in one of the national parks. When it came in September 1999, we were scrambling to respond to the many requests for help which by then were beginning to arrive almost weekly and so we sent a less than encouraging reply. We explained that someone from the international team would need to make an initial visit to spend time with the group he had put together. That would be the only way we could know if their ideas could add up to a viable A Rocha project, but such a visit would take time to organise. At present, not only had we no funds for new travel but we had no capacity to accompany them through a proper induction process into the wider A Rocha family of national organisations.

We have never discovered if this discouraging reply went missing or whether it seemed to Moses to be rather lacking in faith, but three months later we got his second email announcing with great rejoicing that A Rocha Ghana had now completed its registration with the government as an environmental NGO. A Rocha Ghana was born – amen!

After some further exchanges, he very graciously deregistered the organisation, even though by then some of the country's senior scientists such as the botanist Professor Alfred Oteng-Yeboah and church leaders such as Robert Oboagye-Mensah, were actively involved, along with students from several colleges and universities. For the next three years, while we gathered the resources to make the organisational relationships mean something, they carried on with a number of student-led initiatives under the name of the Eden Conservation Society. Finally, in 2003, David Payne was able to visit with another of our international Trustees, Bihini Won wa Musiti from the Democratic Republic of Congo. Bihini and David had both had experience with many projects throughout Africa over the last three decades, but even by their exacting standards, what they saw in Ghana was very impressive. So they encouraged Theresa Maa Ohui Ayiku, who was running operations in Accra, to join us for the Leaders' Forum in Portugal in July so that she could meet the rest of the A Rocha family and hear that they could now become A Rocha Ghana with the full blessing of the international Trustees.

One of their early projects had been sited around the Mole National Park in the north of the country. It soon attracted international support as an illustration of the way that A Rocha as a Christian organisation could often bring new approaches to bear on old problems, particularly in societies where the church plays a major role. Park officials had inherited thirty years of bad feeling that went back to the exclusion of local people from the protected area when it was first established. Nearly all of those now living in the villages around the park were members of churches so there was a natural context for the new A Rocha team to begin work. Their challenge was to create sustainable livelihoods for the local communities that didn't put at risk the highly endangered habitats of the park which provided the only long-term hope for the survival of people and animals alike. Chief among the initial projects have been bee-keeping, tuition in dry season gardening and the introduction of low cost technology for shea butter extraction from the valuable endemic woodlands. Tree planting has recently become an additionally important activity as part of the new A Rocha carbon reduction programme, Climate Stewards.[2]

Climate Stewards was the initiative of an emerging group of business people who are contributing their talents and energy to A Rocha. Once again it went from being a bright idea to a real project making a difference in several different countries through a highly sacrificial gift of volunteer time. In this case it came from David Hughes who had just retired, and Jenny Bowles who laid down the opportunity to do a PhD in order to become the Program Manager (unpaid – which is the word that really deserves the capital letter). Shortly afterwards, they were joined by Jenny's husband Brendan, ensuring penury for the entire family. For me, Brendan's arrival in A Rocha was the culmination of a twenty-five year campaign to find a way for him to join us, started after he gave us a beautiful design for our very first leaflet in 1983. The Climate Stewards team wanted to find a practical way to link the lifestyle of the northern hemisphere with its impact in the south, and it was that concern which gave them the necessary commitment and drive to get through the huge amount of work that was needed as the business began. A similar awareness also motivated the emerging A Rocha group in the Netherlands.

As one might expect of the Dutch, the beginnings of their national organisation were quite measured. It came about through a series of highly organised initiatives undertaken by journalists Embert and Petra Messelink who had been invited to visit A Rocha France by Petra Crofton. (I hope by now you were prepared for another Petra.) Her idea was that they and their three small children might help run Les Tourades during the team's summer break; she suspected that they would be instantly captivated by the vision. They were: it seemed to be the ideal way that they could combine Embert's love for birding and new expressions of the Christian faith with Petra's calling to community. But, as they returned home and began to share their hopes for a project with friends, they seemed to be constantly confronted by what we came to know as 'the Dutch question'. In brief, it asked why A Rocha was necessary at all in a country with thousands of environmental groups and equal numbers of churches. Over the last three decades or more, there had been quite a few Christian environmental initiatives, but most had eventually run out of steam and Embert and Petra found it difficult to encounter much enthusiasm for another attempt.

However, they were convinced that a project rooted in action, which wholeheartedly took on the passions of both

Christians and environmental people (who were by now quite divided parties), could make an important contribution. They also believed that an A Rocha Netherlands group could mobilise hundreds of skilled people to go to help other A Rocha projects. They were proved right almost immediately and Dutch groups soon began to arrive in other countries. I cannot now think of any A Rocha centre that has not already benefited from their cheerful expertise.

Ironically, their own field study centre has been a long time coming but, at the time of writing, it seems the frustrating wait may soon be over. Once again, that will be their story so I leave it there for now. However, Embert and Petra soon ran up against the other perennial question that is part of any A Rocha narrative, 'How on earth will we fund it all?'

Chapter Fourteen:

Cash or Kind

Money cannot buy
The fuel of love:
But is excellent kindling.[1]

W.H. Auden

The issue of money, taboo in some cultures and insufficiently so in others, came to the fore at the outset of A Rocha's life. In 1982, when we first proposed the idea of a Christian field study centre to the head of the sonorously named Bible Churchmen's Missionary Society (now Crosslinks), their General Secretary, John Ball, sent us a pastoral reply which spelled out the terms under which they could give us some support. He told us that if we wanted to see A Rocha established, then we would need to shoulder the responsibility for seeing it funded, and that recognition has been a part of our working lives ever since.

The challenge of fundraising has given rise to a great deal of heart-searching and, at times, more despair and exhilaration than almost any other issue. I say 'almost' because I have found that nothing in my working life costs me sleep like the inevitable rough moments in relationships that come whenever you work with fellow human beings. Financial struggles are a breeze by comparison.

While many manuals and how-to guides exist, it seems that almost nothing has been published on what Henri Nouwen called 'the spirituality of fundraising', so we have found little guidance available for the issues that have troubled us most. They have had less to do with working out how to raise money, than with the questions, 'How can we live calmly alongside a set of urgent needs?' 'If a lack of funds could mean we risk failure, what happens to our relationships with our colleagues?' 'Should we ask our personal friends to support the work we now care about so passionately?' 'If we go to meet people primarily to ask for financial support, how can we live the relationship with integrity?' And because anyone who fundraises soon ends up passing on part of what they raise, 'What is it going to mean for our relationships with those that we help?'

A first answer to many of these questions was to do all we could to manage A Rocha's finances and our own family finances too, by the truth that God cares far more about who we are than what we do. The second answer began with our understanding that although faith is for the massive challenges of life and death, trusting God also translates into the most mundane of circumstances. For many of us throughout most of our lives, it is worked out in a very complex world that is simultaneously charged with suffering and glory.

So as A Rocha's financial decisions were made, we knew we were dealing with something profoundly spiritual and significant for the whole character of the organisation, and not merely with operational procedures. As investigative journalist Bob Woodward tried to get to the truth of the Watergate cover-up he was given the classic advice, 'Follow the money'. We have discovered it isn't a bad guide to where the truth will be found in Christian or environmental organisations too. A careful look at how they spend their money will usually tell you what they really care about and where their heart is.

The importance we attach to relationships explains a lot about our international budget. Helping people to work together well costs money and, when essential training is added to the equation, the expense is considerable. As a result, we have all needed to find creative ways to bring in the required support. But the vision for the organisation comes first: only then do we give our efforts to writing a budget and working for the money to turn convictions into reality.

If our secular donors have had a hard time understanding A Rocha budgets which demonstrate that human relationships are central to how we work, our Christian supporters have sometimes struggled to understand the need for rigorous, and so sometimes expensive, methodology in our field projects. But it has been very worthwhile to make the explanations to both constituencies. For our own part, financial shortages have taught us to value the process of doing good work as much as the satisfaction of completing it. We have learned from our colleagues in Lebanon and elsewhere that it is also the best way to survive the strains of working in the more unpredictable and volatile contexts in which we increasingly find ourselves.

If how we do things is what truly matters, then A Rocha's work, in itself, should carry meaning. It will certainly speak far more loudly about who we are and what we care about than anything we can say. However, if our choices raise questions, then we need to take time for more listening and more explanations. If we spend hard-raised

and generously given money on equipment to weigh warblers or on building conduits to measure water quality it is
because we believe a number of things. We believe our data
can contribute to the survival of the habitats and species we
are studying, and so it must be accurate. We believe that the
survival of species is important, that scientific enquiry is
valid, and that truth itself matters. We believe that our work
for the care of the non-human creation is important to its
Creator – the list is almost endless. But we have reasons for
all these beliefs, and our discussions with potential donors
have often been worthwhile because they have enabled us
to talk freely about what we all really care about. It is often
when these fundamental questions have been aired that we
get to talking about the more familiar and programmatic
ones such as 'How are projects sustainable long-term
really?' or 'If you say projects only really work if the local
communities are involved from the start, how do you make
that happen?' Perhaps it is because money is so important
to us all that fundraising conversations are nearly always
an exchange of beliefs. It is certainly why fundraising is
about far more than simply trying to raise money and why
it is an inherently spiritual activity.

Whenever people discover that working with A Rocha is
going to involve them in raising money, it nearly always
causes initial hesitation and many questions. But after
much discussion, we are coming to believe that everyone,
from whatever country or culture they come, will benefit
from looking for some kind of personal support. Once
again we have found there is no blueprint to follow. There
are many ways of finding funds that range from applying
for highly technical government grants to asking for personal donations and gifts. The important issue is that our

search for support always brings others into the orbit of our work. It can be the way for a wider community of people to get involved in what we are doing even if they can't give anything themselves. Support is not just about money; it can be even more precious when it comes in the form of time, or prayer, or equipment. Neither is it about simple monetary value: a bicycle loaned in Ghana can make as much difference to the success of a project as a car given in Europe.

I recently learned a good lesson about being less complicated in asking for support from film director Melissa Ong, who joined our team in 2005. She and her husband Daniel Tay were working in the Singaporean film industry, but they were searching for a way of applying their skills to the service of both conservation and Christian mission. Their church was giving them little encouragement and they were just beginning to believe the quest would be impossible when they found A Rocha on the internet.

'Do you have a media department?' asked her first email.

'No, but would you be interested in starting one?' was my reply, along with the usual rider that we would be unable to provide any funding to help them. They refused to see the idea as far-fetched, and by living very sacrificially while making their need for support known to all their friends, they have gone on to donate three years to A Rocha, producing a powerful series of short films. Their footage has given its own vivid appreciation of what the different teams are doing and, from their home within the Canadian team, they have now introduced thousands of new people around the world to A Rocha – it has been a true gift to us all.

But early in the adventure, Mel was with me in London

as we went to talk to a donor who we hoped might be interested in supporting them. Just before we knocked on his door I heard her say in her typically clipped and gnomic Singlish, 'Ask for a donkey.' There was no time for her to explain this mysterious remark further and, despite my growing respect for her wisdom, I resisted the temptation to take her literally. As we left after what proved to be a fruitless conversation with our donor (but at least with no donkey) she told me what she meant – she had been reading how Jesus prepared for his entry into Jerusalem by sending his friends to ask for help, and it had given her a great biblical precedent.

As we talked it over we realised it was one of many – we see Jesus requesting water at the well and asking for start-up supplies in a crisis when 5,000 people had to be fed. We read Paul's letter urging the wealthier churches to send what they could spare to the poorer ones, and find accounts of the early Christian community spontaneously sharing their wealth alongside a record of their more hard-hearted members' deceit and shame. Biblical characters in extremity find what they need in other paradoxical episodes: Elijah asks for help from a destitute widow and is provided for; Elisha is looked after, without asking, by a wealthy couple. Even creation itself plays a part in miraculous provision in the form of bread-bearing ravens and net-breaking shoals of fish.

Apart from ravens and fish I would say that we have benefited from almost every kind of giving during twenty-five years of finding support for A Rocha. Although the effort has frequently been accompanied by much perplexity, the biggest mystery of all is that the work seems to go forward year after year, despite a frequent lack of funding.

At so many critical moments (or, more typically, after what we believe to have been critical moments), the money has either been provided or has proved not to be needed.

To make this personal, I need to confess that I am temperamentally anxious and am locked in a lifelong battle to tame a raging impatience. So the truth is that I have yet to arrive at a point where I can live this process peacefully. The Lord's sense of timing seems to have more in common with Miranda's and to share her Irish sense of pace, rather than doing justice to my own ideas of what is urgent. My instincts were originally Anglo-Saxon and are now undoubtedly mongrel, but either way they don't seem to have given me the patience that I so sorely need to live A Rocha's finances calmly. What I have come to realise is that when once our requests have been made as professionally as resources allow, if no support is forthcoming, my only remaining argument is with the wisdom of God and there I must leave it. Miranda and I have often suggested to those who have joined us in A Rocha's essentially insecure adventures that it seems that a lack of funds has frequently been God's chosen way of getting his message across to us. It has never normally been a lack of money that has prevented what we intend from coming about, but rather a lack of wise intentions. If, as C.S. Lewis famously implied, suffering can be 'God's megaphone' to our deaf souls, then financial stress can be his hearing aid for deaf Christian enterprises.

The early decision to have no headquarters has equipped us well for life with limited finances and has allowed the maximum amount of funding to be applied to field projects. We have been meeting only three or four times a year but, with a team of about twenty people now, we have recently become too numerous even to do that. A stop press moment occurred in the writing of these pages with the arrival of Marie Connett Porceddu as our new Chief Executive Officer: one of the first things the Trustees have asked her to do is to review how we can now operate as a larger organisation. After only a few months of her leadership, it is clear that she approaches any challenge like that by looking for strategic answers that reflect our understanding of God and that do justice to our relationships with each other and the creation.

We have also been better fitted to ride the high and low tides of project funding by our other decision to endeavour to find some of our personal support. Different people have found different ways to meeting the challenge of making their work financially viable as they join the international team, but Rob and Kathy Thomas approached it in a particularly courageous fashion.

'We knew we had to be self-funded,' Rob wrote shortly after they joined the team in 2003, 'so we sold our house which paid off the mortgage. That meant we were able to buy a cheaper house in Nottingham to provide a base for our daughters who were studying there and they were very supportive of the decision! Both of us have given up salaried jobs, but I am still working one day a week as a consultant for my old firm of solicitors. We're probably living on half the income we had before.' They then moved into two rooms upstairs in the A Rocha centre in Southall as its first managers, beginning by leading the task of converting it from its rundown state as a former nursing home to become a fully equipped centre. After its major overhaul, the house has provided a fine base for the growing number of volunteers and team members and has given the national organisation some essential office space.

Over the next three years they welcomed hundreds of people to the centre, together with Dave and Anne and the family who were living just two doors further down the street. As well as Rob's database expertise, Kathy's artistic skills and their joint commitment to creating a community, they gave us all a remarkable example of the difference that can be made by undemonstrative, but quietly radical, choices. They also proved that in a pioneer situation it is always wise to sit loosely to your job description as in the event their work was far less international than anyone had anticipated. But Rob and Kathy's sense of calling carried them through, as it has sustained all of those who have joined A Rocha teams with a readiness to take on whatever work was most important. It has also taken them through the challenges of living without long-term guarantees of funding, or much certainty of what the future might hold.

Even though they rarely left the UK, living in Southall meant that they became aware of another major issue with which we have all had to come to terms during this decade of very rapid growth: the unconscious domination of Anglo-Saxon ways of doing things. I referred to it briefly in an earlier chapter because it easily becomes hard-wired into many international organisations and we are no exception. Whenever all our leaders from around the world are together, we are frequently and painfully aware that this bias can easily influence not just what we decide is impor-tant to discuss but even the way we set up the exchanges themselves. Both can reveal hidden assumptions and it takes wisdom and hard work to make an event work well for over seventy people from more than twenty countries.

For some of our African leaders the way into any dis-cussion needs to come from the oldest ones present, in the form of a set piece introduction. Only then can the contribution of their younger colleagues follow and be validated. While individually-minded Westerners welcome heated discussions, our Asian colleagues prefer a quiet consensus to emerge. Large groups enable some to express what they think and small groups are the only possible forum for others. We are learning to build all these preferences into the way we make our decisions.

We have also discovered that one of the best ways to understand each other is to see how we lead worship. We never cease to be astonished by the wealth of difference in how we all approach Christ in this most personal and communal of times. Vijay and Prem from India will take off their shoes as they come forward to lead our praying; Kip from Kenya feels that a communal shout can draw us all together; and silence can be very appealing to the Westerner coming to worship after his hyperactive week of too many meetings and too much travel.

As we are in worship, in our place before God in spirit and in truth, so we are most profoundly known.

Chapter Fifteen:

Hope for the Planet

The creation waits in eager expectation for the [children] of God to be revealed.

Paul's Epistle to the Romans, chapter 8 verse 19
(my brackets)

'How do you deal with the heartbreak?' The question came from a zoology graduate confronted with the reality of widespread habitat devastation and species extinction.

He told me that he had been completely unable to come to terms with what he was learning, so had opted to change track and study theology as a safer option. But any true reading of the biblical theology will lead us into an even greater involvement with life on earth, so rather than finding he had embarked on a kind of religious retreat, he found himself facing the question again.

He argued that the current state of affairs offers a bleak outlook for anyone who cares about God's creation. Most studies show that we now have very little time left to protect the more vulnerable species and yet they account for nearly a quarter of the global total. The task is made infinitely more complex by our rapidly changing climate and the highly damaging impact that the new conditions are having on human and non-human life. Furthermore, many argue that even if we were to make the essential, radical changes to safeguard biodiversity and human well-being, they would not be enough to reverse many of the more alarming trends.

It seemed as we talked that he was wrestling with the problem of suffering. Even if he was facing it in an ecological context it was an age-old theological question that always affects us deeply and personally. How can we understand the persistent presence of pain and evil if we believe in a loving God? Human suffering is bad enough but my questioner was feeling the suffering of creation itself – what the apostle Paul calls its 'groaning' – and was finding it truly heartbreaking. Just as the person at the bedside of a terminally ill friend is distressed, so those truly attentive to the destruction and pollution of the earth ask how God, who is 'loving towards all he has made', can permit it all. For the ecologist who is a Christian, the devastations that have been wrought in the world in consequence of our broken human relationship with God seem to reach into the fabric of every ecosystem, and it can be very hard to bear.

As the devastations now visited on the earth are most keenly felt by the poorest of the poor, so directly affected by their environment, the question is also about justice. Such catastrophe seems entirely out of keeping with our sense of what God intends.

Both of these questions rapidly translate into a further one that is more pastoral. It was exemplified in the experience of another student at the same college who was battling with the emotional toll of apparent failure after a lifetime spent studying amphibians.

During lunch one day, he took an hour to tell me of the

extraordinary discoveries he had made and of how he had come to appreciate the incredible complexities of the species he was studying. He had learned that some of his frogs were expert botanists: they would seek out particular plants where their favourite bees came to feed and then hide just below their leaves, leaping out to grab the insects as they flew past. Others knew the little wind and water currents of the pools so well that they were able to ambush dragonflies when they lost height over the water at particular times of day. Many of the small ponds on his study site held similar secrets and he had made observations that were quite new. Although he was sure that such insights would have been granted to anyone who took the time to watch and listen carefully, it was clear that his studies had given him unique knowledge of a remarkable ecosystem.

His years of patient observation came to a sudden halt one spring morning as his site and everything in it was randomly destroyed by illegal water pumping for a nearby road building programme. Years afterwards he still carried an intense sadness and frustration at this abrupt end to years of patient work and even more at the summary destruction of such a special place.

He, like many others, had come to believe that the life, death and resurrection of Christ give us a starting point for understanding the theological and pastoral questions that we face as we witness the ongoing destruction of God's earth. The life of Christ was the most material of stories – a poverty-stricken birth into a political shambles, a refugee childhood, a politically oppressed youth and brief, controversial adult years that ended in violent execution. But his resurrection is recounted in equally material terms: Jesus invites Thomas to touch his wounds and then goes on to eat fish on the beach with his baffled disciples. What blazes through the account of Jesus' life on earth is the presence of God. All creation is drawn into the agony of his death as darkness falls and the earth shudders. His resurrection proclaims an unquenchable hope amid apparently random suffering: a new way had begun which would transform and transcend all of the governing realities.

As we face our own acute environmental challenges, nothing has changed about the nature of Christian hope. There are things we see and things we don't. The work of those who care for creation will never be a succession of conservation victories, any more than the work of medics will lead to the final eradication of disease. We are unlikely to find that we suddenly have abundant resources to make visible and significant changes that will renew life on the earth. We are not going to be spared from effects of the multiform brokenness of this world, even while science allows us greater knowledge of all that it means for the fabric of life.

What we can see are the loving purposes of God in the earth's very making and sustaining. As we ourselves respond in ways he provides, so we understand better that he is far more committed to creation's restoration and renewal than we could ever be. We are promised his wisdom for our work and his hope to guide us to good solutions. Both can make an intensely practical difference to each working day.

There is nothing escapist in this. While prayer allows us to see something of the wider purposes of our Creator, it also prompts us to take the part of a suffering creation and to be drawn into its acute stress. As I write, news has been arriving from our first study site on the Alvor estuary of yet more illegal destruction and, even after twenty-five years of work, we still have no guarantee that its habitats will survive the assault. No recognition that God graces his creation with his presence, that his fire is in every Kingfisher, can protect us from ongoing struggles, or allow us to define success on our own terms.

These pages have recounted some of the ways in which we have been called to be part of the sustaining mission of God's Spirit. The resurrection of Jesus lies at the heart of what understanding we have of our task. What has kept us going through the set-backs and mysteries is knowing that we are a tiny part of a total and loving redemption that has already begun but which will only come to final completion at a time beyond our understanding. The glimpses we have gained of that redemption, in the partially restored forest and communities around Kenya's Mida Creek, the renewed Lebanese wetlands of Aammiq, the changed London landscape at Minet, and in many thousands of encounters with people who themselves have been part of the work of restoration, constantly renew our hope.

There is a full and redemptive circle here. It was God's intention that humanity, made in the image of God, might be creation-keepers. As we are renewed in Christ to become his body now, so we return to that original calling. As the extremely poor Christian communities around Ghana's Mole National Park have begun to play their part in the renewal of the park itself, so they have been given new livelihoods by the restoration of the woodlands. The care of creation opens a way of transformation and hope for each of us. We can begin to drink water thankfully, to breathe with gratitude. In every place we find ourselves, in creative or mundane ways, there are opportunities close at hand for the restoration of a despoiled creation.

Further hope lies in the real possibility that the world-wide church will recover its earth-keeping vocation. If Christians in the wealthy West abandon their addiction to consumption without bounds the impact will be felt around the planet. If stewardship becomes a normal part of life in Christ for believers in the tropical areas where biodiversity is concentrated, extraordinary changes could be seen. It will take a new sense of God-given responsibility, but a recovered understanding of similar global responsibilities has changed the church in previous ages. If our new vocation can inform all the others we already embrace, then something very significant may be seen.

Other tides might turn in unexpected ways. Even the remarkable growth of the Christian church in China could be seen as a sign of environmental hope in a country that has witnessed some of the worst instances of ecological degradation anywhere on earth. We might pray that the many believers who are now active at all levels of Chinese society may find good reason in their faith to respond to the current environmental crises. If, even in their frequent trials, they can demonstrate a different way of life, it could be a sign to wider Chinese society of something far more compelling than the narrow economic logic which has led to such widespread destruction.

It seems that in many parts of China there is already a growing recognition of how the natural resources that are needed to create a more prosperous society cannot be treated with indifference. At the same time, there are indications of a wider interest in the contribution that Christian thinking made to the rise of capitalism and Western prosperity. From there it will be a short step to engaging with questions of sustainability as climate change and the impacts of pollution begin to make themselves more acutely felt throughout the country.

It will be ironic if it is left to Chinese believers to alert their Western counterparts to the missing component of stewardship in the history of our faith. As the industrial revolution gained momentum in eighteenth-century Europe there was little biblical reflection on the consequences for creation, with sobering consequences. We ourselves have seen similar ironies and have learned to find our hope in unexpected places: recent partnerships between A Rocha and organisations such as Conservation International and IUCN (The World Conservation Union) have helped us greatly, even with the task of persuading our fellow Christians of the urgent need to care for creation.

The first two generations of national A Rocha organisations have now gained real impetus and maturity. New projects have been established in Brazil, New Zealand and Uganda during the writing of these last few chapters and we know of Christians in a dozen other countries from Nepal to Benin, Mozambique and Papua New Guinea who would join us tomorrow if resources allowed. Christians all over the world now have the care of creation as second nature in their daily life in Christ, whether they work in business or farming, medicine or teaching. The Kingfisher's fire is lighting up streams all over the world.

This book has told a story which is developing by the day. The account which ends here is offered in homage to the sheer courage and persistence of all who have been involved, most of whom have gone without mention. They are a true example of hope for God's earth.

End Notes

Acknowledgements

1. Barbara and Richard Mearns, *John Kirk Townsend,* Dumfries 2007. See www.mearnsbooks.com

Prologue

1. First published, Hodder and Stoughton, London 1993. Now, Regent College Publishing, Vancouver BC.

2. Eugene H Peterson, *Christ Plays in Ten Thousand Places*, Eerdmans, Grand Rapids, 2005.

Chapter One: The Landscape

1 Robert Bridges, ed. *Poems of Gerard Manley Hopkins*, Poem 41, Oxford, UK: Oxford University Press, 1931.

2 Paul Theroux, *Dark Star Safari*, London: Penguin Books, 2002, page 177.

3 http://www.grist.org/news/maindish/2006/10/17/wilson/index.html.

4 An Urgent Call to Action: Scientists and Evangelicals Unite to Protect Creation, 17 January, 2007. http://chge.med.harvard.edu/media/releases/jan_17.html

5 http://www.grist.org/news/maindish/2006/10/17/wilson/index.html.

6 James Jones, *Jesus and the Earth*, London: SPCK, 2003.

7 David Bebbington, *Evangelicalism in Modern Britain: A History from the 1730s to the 1980s*, Grand Rapids, MI: Baker, 1992.

8 http://www.christianitytoday.com/bc/2005/006/17.17.html.

9 An Urgent Call to Action: Scientists and Evangelicals Unite to Protect Creation, 17 January, 2007.

10 Lynn White, 'The Historical Roots of our Ecologic Crisis', *Science*, vol. 155 (Number 3767), 10 March 1967, pages, 1203-1207. For

comprehensive discussions of White's ideas see Iain Provan, Earth-keeping and People Keeping in the Old Testament, *Crux* magazine, Regent College, Vancouver, summer 2006, vol. 42, no. 2.

11 Fred van Dyke, 'Cultural transformation and conservation: growth, influences and challenges for the Judeo-Christian stewardship environmental ethic', *Perspectives on Science and Christian Faith*, 58:48-63, 2006.

12 T.S. Eliot, Four Quartets. East Coker, *Collected Poems*, London: Faber and Faber Ltd., 2002.

Chapter Two: Picking Up the Portuguese Story

1 Rose Macauley, on George Borrow, *They Went to Portugal*, Jonathan Cape, London: Penguin, 1985, page 182.

Chapter Three: New Beginnings and Early Dying

1 David Jones, *In Parenthesis*, London: Faber and Faber Ltd., 1937.

Chapter Four: Under African Skies

1 Ryszard Kapuscinski, *The Shadow of the Sun*, London: Penguin, 2001.

2 His mother Rachel's book about Pete's life and death is an inspiring account. *Pete's Story*, Milton Keynes, UK: Authentic Media, 2006

Chapter Five: Beirut, the Bekaa and Beyond

1 H.B. Tristram, *The Land of Israel. A Journal of Travels in Palestine*, London: Society for Promoting Christian Knowledge, 1865.

Chapter Six: The Heart of the Question

1 Quoted in Simon Brett, ed., *Faber Book of Diaries 1987*, from Barclay Fox's Journal, London, Bell and Hyman, 1979.

2 *Crux* magazine, spring 2006, Regent College, Vancouver. Report of the World Commission on Environment and Development, *Brundtland Commission*, Our Common Future, United Nations General Assembly, 4 August 1987, 40, Doc A/43/427. Also, Oxford University Press, 1987

3 One of the more alarming of these studies, the Global Amphibian Assessment, was led by one of our own trustees, Simon Stuart, in the course of his day job for Conservation International/ IUCN.

4 See the Millennium Ecosystem Assessment: www.millenniu-massessment.org/.

5 2 Corinthians 4:4, NIV.

6 Curtis White, *Orion* Magazine March/April 2007.

7 Gordon Fee, Exegesis of Romans 8 at the A Rocha/Regent College 'Creation Groaning' conference 2003 reporting on Professor Marguerte Shuster's work reported at a St Joseph's Seminary New York exegetical conference, April 2003. One of the sermons was by Spurgeon.

8 John Stott, *Balanced Christianity*, London: Hodder & Stoughton, 1975.

9 *New York Times* article by Michael Luo and Laurie Goodstein 21 May 2007.

10 Lt Gen Romeo Dallaire, *Shake Hands with the Devil*, London: Arrow Books, 2004, pages 517, 519.

Chapter Seven: The French Exception

1 Robert Morley, *Musing Morley: Selected Writings*, London: Coronet Books, 1981.

2. Jo Swinney, *Through The Dark Woods*, Monarch, Oxford, 2007

Chapter Eight: Change from Inside

1 W.H. Auden, *Collected Poems*, London: Faber and Faber Ltd., 1976.

2 Acts chapter 17.

3 Acts 17:21-23.

4
http://w01.international.gc.ca/minpub/Publication.asp?publication_id=378081&Language=E.

5 Bill Rees, who developed the Ecological Footprint analyses at University of British Columbia, Vancouver, Canada citing UN-HDR 2005 figures at Regent College, March 2007.

6 The illness is caused from the natural mineral contamination of groundwater, formerly inaccessible, but now widely used after the massive development effort to sink boreholes that now supply over 50

million people in Bangladesh alone. http://www.bangladesh.net/article_bangladesh/health/hlt_02_arsenicosi.htm.

7 http://www.un.org/esa/population/publications/wup2001/WUP2001-pressrelease.pdf.

8 1 Corinthians 12:27.

9 Acts 17:24, NIV.

10 Acts 17:26, TNIV

11 Hosea 4:1-3, NIV.

12 I am grateful to J.I. Packer for his introduction to George Whitefield's list of questions in his article 'Self-Care for Pastors' in *Crux* magazine, December 2003, vol. 39, no. 4.

13. Acts 17:25, TNIV

Chapter Nine: Common Ground in Southall

1 Bill McKibben, Deep Economy: *The Wealth of Communities and the Durable Future*, Times Books, New York, 2007. See also http://www.amacad.org/publications/fall2001/mckibben.aspx.

2 *Anglicans for Renewal*, vol 62.

3 Dave and Anne Bookless, provisional title: *Passion for the Planet*, UK: A Rocha, 2008.

Chapter Ten: Why Theology Matters to Tree Frogs

1 Christopher Smart, *Collected Poems*, Fyfield Books, Manchester, 1979, page 49.

2 I am grateful to Professor Sir Ghillean Prance for these notes from Maurice Strong's Environmental Lecture at the Royal Botanical Gardens, Kew, 1993.

3 http://www.thebreakthrough.org/images/Death_of_Environmentalism.pdf.

4 http://www.millenniumassessment.org. The Millennium Ecosystem Assessment assessed the consequences of ecosystem change for human well-being. From 2001 to 2005, the MA involved the work of more than 1,360 experts worldwide. Their findings provide a state-of-the-art scientific appraisal of the condition and trends in the world's ecosystems and the services they provide, as well as the scientific basis for action to conserve and use them sustainably.

5 Colossians 1:16-17.

6 Personal comment, A Rocha Brazil conference, November 2006.

7 http://www.biodiversityhotspots.org.

8 Max Oelschlager, *Caring for Creation: An Ecumenical Approach to the Environmental Crisis*, New Haven and London: Yale University Press, 1994.

9 Titles such as Fred Van Dyke, David C. Mahan, Joseph K. Sheldon, Raymond H. Brand, *Redeeming Creation: The Biblical Basis for Environmental Stewardship*, Downers Grove, IL: InterVarsity, 1996.

Chapter Eleven: New Worlds

1 W.H. Auden, *Collected Poems*, London: Faber and Faber Ltd., 1976.

2 Virginia Vroblesky, *The Gift of Creation: a discussion guide on caring for the environment*, Colorado Springs: NavPress, 1992.

3 *Conservation Biology,* vol. 19, no. 2, April 2005, pages 290-292.

4 *Conservation Biology*, vo1. 19, no. 6, December 2005, pages 1689-1692.

5 http://www.news.harvard.edu/gazette/2000/11.09/11-nature.html.

6 J. Matthew Sleeth, MD, *Serve God Save the Planet*, Grand Rapids, MI: Zondervan, 2006. For more of their story, also see www.servegod-savetheplanet.org

Chapter Twelve: Going Global

1 Wendell Berry, *Another Turn of the Crank,* Washington DC: Counterpoint Press, 1995, page 12.

Chapter Thirteen: The Turning Tide on Many Shores

1 US Defence Secretary, press conference, February 2002.

2 www.climatestewards.net

Chapter Fourteen: Cash or Kind

1 W.H. Auden, *Collected Poems*, London: Faber and Faber Ltd., 1976.

Contact Information

A Rocha International
3 Hooper St
Cambridge
CB1 2NZ
UK

international@arocha.org
www.arocha.org

A Rocha UK
13 Avenue Road
Southall
Middlesex
UB1 3BL

uk@arocha.org